The
VIEWFINDER
Michael's Story

MICHAEL J. BOWEN

Anchors Publishing, Wilmington, North Carolina
© 2026 Michael J. Bowen
Bowen, Michael J., 1962
The Viewfinder: Michael's Story/Michael J. Bowen
Original trade paperback ISBN-13: 9798985126419
ebook ISBN-13: 9798985126433
Original trade hardcover ISBN-13: 9798985126457
Library of Congress Control Number: 2021923669

This book is a memoir. The stories in this book reflect the author's recollection of events. The dialogue in the book has been re-created from memory. Some names, locations, and identifying characteristics have been changed to protect the privacy of those depicted.

Book & cover design by James Slate
Edited by Jennifer Huston Schaeffer of White Dog Editorial Services.
Jacket author photograph by Kaitlin Bucci Photography

All rights reserved. No part of this book may be reproduced, displayed, modified, or distributed by any means (electronic, mechanical, photocopying, recording, or otherwise) without the express prior written permission of the copyright holder, with the exception of brief quotations included in reviews.

For further information and permissions approval or to order copies of this book, go to www.anchorspublishing.com

Second Printing, 2026
Printed in the United States of America

Dedicated to Betty and "Bo" Bowen, whose house was welcoming to all. Who showed me and my brother that growing up without the best things in life was the best thing for us.

PREFACE

For thirty-five years, I told myself that no one would want to read a book about what happened to me, someone who is "imperfect" in every way. I didn't see how my story would serve others and serve God. So, for many years, *The Viewfinder* remained nothing more than a verbal diary that I started recording as therapy in March 1986.

In 1991, I converted my recordings into a manuscript titled *Working Hard at Being Happy*. Frustrated with my inability to express my thoughts on paper, I tucked away my partially written manuscript with no plans to finish it. However, in early 2008, after losing my mom to cancer, I was inspired to finish the long-forgotten memoir as a tribute to my mother's lifelong sacrifices for our family. A year later, it was complete. But as a "thinking introvert" who is always pensive and introspective, I concluded that my manuscript was unworthy of becoming a book. So, for a second time, I put my story away.

Fast-forward a decade later and this time, it was my dad whose health was declining. During a weekend visit with him at my childhood home in Washington

PREFACE

Park, North Carolina, I happened upon two items that made me rethink the dynamic of my memoir and would end up playing significant roles in my story: a stuffed lion that I found collecting dust in my bedroom closet and a ceramic mug that sat upon the mantel of the fireplace in my parents' kitchen. Staring at the dates painted on the mug (11-19-1985 to 2-21-1986) transported me back to February 21, 1986, where I sat in a wheelchair clutching a stuffed lion named Arnold, who represented courage. I vividly recalled the gamut of emotions I felt on that February day more than thirty years earlier. The harrowing events I experienced between November of 1985 and February of 1986 forever changed my life. Sitting there in the kitchen of my parents' house, I realized that my story was worth telling. But I wanted to tell it in the present tense so readers could experience, in actual time, what happened to me starting on that fateful day in November 1985 and how the Holy Spirit transformed my personality.

So, for a third time, I brought my manuscript out of retirement. But this time before I rewrote it, I asked God to give me the inspiration to write a book that would glorify him and also allow me to tell my unique story. Ultimately, the title of my book and the life lessons learned emerged during this rewrite. *The Viewfinder* recounts the trials, tribulations, and triumphs I experienced after suffering a spinal cord injury in a car accident at the age of twenty-three. This is my story.

THE VIEWFINDER

CHAPTER 1

IT'S QUARTER AFTER SIX on the morning of November 19, 1985, and I'm at my girlfriend Sharon's apartment sitting on a barstool while she puts the finishing touches on my makeup. She and her roommates have teamed up to dress me for my role as a transvestite in Arnold Schwarzenegger's latest movie, *Raw Deal*. I step in front of the full-length mirror and laugh at my appearance. I'm not sure what a transvestite is supposed to look like, but Sharon has teased my shoulder-length, dirty-blond hair and applied a heavy coat of mascara to my eyelashes. I'm wearing black spandex leggings with a silver-studded belt, a matching choker and wristbands, and a skintight, sleeveless, black T-shirt that belongs to one of Sharon's girlfriends. An acid washed jean jacket tops off my outfit.

Dubbed "Hollywood East," the city of Wilmington has recently become home to Screen Gem Studios, and a burgeoning film industry is quickly taking root. Actors that come to the area draw little attention from residents, and the stars like it that way. Occasionally, recruiters from the production company De Laurentiis

CHAPTER 1

Entertainment Group, visit the campus of UNC–Wilmington looking for students to be movie extras, and yesterday, I was in the right place at the right time.

However, the more Sharon and her roommates compliment my appearance, the more I start to think I'm going to make a huge fool of myself. On my way to the shoot at a downtown nightclub, I begin second-guessing myself and wonder if the fifty dollars I'm supposed to make today has caused me to have a lapse in judgment. It doesn't help that the combination of my outfit and the car I'm driving is generating double takes from other drivers.

The 1966 Volkswagen Beetle was a Christmas gift from my brother, Lee, a couple of years earlier. He transformed it into a "Baja Bug" by adding Baja fenders and removing the rear engine compartment. To add a touch of originality, the bug is painted canary yellow with a multicolored stripe that begins at the roof then makes its way down each door panel where it mutates into a lightning bolt. He also decked out the motor in chrome and ensured that the oversize camshaft and three-foot-long header pipe work in unison to belch out an idling sound that only a hot rod enthusiast can appreciate. At a stoplight, the sound of my approach startles an elderly couple in the car next to me. I make eye contact with the lady in the passenger seat, and I can tell by the perplexed expression on her face that she's trying to make sense of what she sees. I nod my head to acknowledge her gaze then shout out the open window, "Hey, how are ya?" This greeting only seems to confuse her more since the deep voice emanating from my mouth doesn't match my heavily made-up appearance. Disconcertedly, she taps her husband on the shoulder then points at me.

He obliges his wife's request and looks in my direction. As we make eye contact, I take my right hand off the steering wheel and give a slight wave. "Good morning," I holler over the roar of the engine. The light turns green, and just before they take off, I regain eye contact with the wife, wink at her, and smile as they pull away.

When I arrive at the nightclub, I ease my car into a parking space across the street. All the extras are congregating in front of the building. As I approach the crowd, I'm taken aback by the costumes some extras are wearing—or, more accurately, the lack thereof. I immediately notice two burly guys standing on the sidewalk dressed in leather jackets and chaps, steel-toed cowboy boots, and Stetson hats. At first, it looks as if they could mount a horse and ride off into the sunset at any moment—until I take a gander at their backsides. It appears that both men forgot to put on their blue jeans before strapping on their chaps. *What have I gotten myself into?* I wonder.

The group recruited for this scene is a smorgasbord of fashion. In front of the nightclub, I notice a gaggle of girls dressed to the nines. Deciding they look to be more my speed, I make my way over to them. "Good morning. How are you, ladies?" I say. The reception to my greeting is lukewarm, so I focus my attention on two girls who acknowledge my existence. Both are rocking leotards, leggings, leg warmers, jean jackets, and stilettos. Aside from the jackets and shoes, they look like they just stepped out of a Jane Fonda aerobics video.

As I strike up a conversation with the girls, the front doors to the nightclub open, and assistants escort us to the dance floor. The director walks on stage and

CHAPTER 1

quiets the crowd of extras. Taking a few minutes to set the scene, he explains that Arnold Schwarzenegger will walk into the club and stop at the bar. As Arnold delivers his lines to the bartender, the music will stop, but the extras are supposed to continue dancing. While at the bar, Arnold will witness the bad guys push a few extras out of the way, then he'll sprint toward them in pursuit. Before the proverbial words *and action*, the director reiterates the importance of continuing to dance once the music stops.

We spend the next five hours working on what can't be more than a sixty-second scene. As he finds one problem after another with the scene, the director grows increasingly frustrated as the hours pass. He randomly removes extras who cannot maintain their rhythm once the music has stopped. The day ends with an announcement for the remaining extras to return the next morning to finish shooting the scene. I accept that my acting days are over and decide not to return.

Many of the extras retire to a makeshift dressing room to change, but I figure I came here in this ridiculous outfit, so what's the harm leaving in it. By the time I leave the nightclub, it's late afternoon and the sun is setting over the Cape Fear River. The walk to my car is chilly as the breeze coming off the river blows right through my thin tights. From Front Street, I turn left onto Orange, which intersects Third, a four-lane road separated by a wide median filled with large oak trees. Parked cars line the right side of Third Street, so in order to cross, I have to ease into the intersection to look for oncoming traffic. When I think the coast is clear, I step on the gas and start making my way through the intersection. I never see the car that strikes my driver's side door. I wasn't wearing my seat belt—it wasn't required back then—so the impact of the crash catapults me into the passenger seat. The passenger door stops the momentum of my lower body, but my head and neck continue on the path of least resistance, shattering the passenger door window. The violent impact knocks me unconscious.

Sometime later, I hear a voice. "Michael . . . Michael, can you hear me? It's Dr. Hatcher. You've been in a wreck. Try not to move. An ambulance is on the way."

Dr. Hatcher is one of my professors at UNC–Wilmington. I'm disoriented and not conscious enough to understand why I hear his voice. *Why is he calling my name?* I think. A loud car horn blares and snaps me out of the fog I'm in. I try to open my eyes but quickly feel excruciating pain, which forces me to close them.

In a moment of clarity, I realize that I've been in a car accident. I cry out, but only a whimper comes out of my mouth. My first thought is that I'm pinned in the car or perhaps underneath it. Panicked, I again scream for help, but it comes out as a raspy whisper. Although I hear Dr. Hatcher telling me it's going to be okay, the quaver in his voice tells me otherwise. Tears well up in my eyes and flow down my cheeks, mixing with blood from the cuts on my face. This cocktail of warm blood, salty tears, and slivers of glass slowly drips down the outer crevice of my nose and into my mouth.

Desperate to know my predicament, I painfully open one eye enough to see. To my relief, I discover that I'm not pinned in the car or underneath it—I'm slouched down in the passenger seat with my arms by my sides. However, my relief quickly

CHAPTER 1

turns to panic when I try to move an arm and then a leg. They remain motionless as if some invisible force is holding them down. At that moment, I realize I'm paralyzed from the neck down, and this reality is more than my conscious mind can cope with.

As the sounds of Dr. Hatcher's voice, the chatter of onlookers, and the busy traffic fade away, I feel myself drifting out of consciousness or perhaps dying. At first, I try to fight it, like a small child attempting to ward off sleep, but the feeling is too intense. It's as if a powerful force is taking control of my mind and placing it in a deep sleep to protect me from my harsh reality.

In this state of unconsciousness, I visit happier times in my life and mischievous moments of my childhood. I relive regretful memories and the impact they had on me and my family. Photos flash in front of my eyes and trigger these memories. Although I'm unconscious, the 3D images feel so real and are so full of depth and vibrant colors that it's like looking through a View-Master. I see an image and immediately relive the experience it depicts. *But why?* I wonder. *Is it my body's way of dissociating itself from an emotional trauma? Sounds logical. Am I dying and this is my life flashing before my eyes? Or does what I'm experiencing hold a deeper meaning? Perhaps the images of my past are being purposefully placed on the reel of this viewfinder not only to comfort me but to teach me some life lessons. That's it! God is holding a divine intervention just for me. . . . What an egotistical thought!*

In the first image I see, I'm maybe four or five years old. I'm standing in front of the bathroom mirror, and Daddy is behind me combing my hair to one side. With a liberal amount of VO5 hair gel on his hands, he works to tame my many cowlicks. He seemed to enjoy this Sunday morning ritual, but I hated it. We would look at each other in the mirror and I'd roll my eyes at Daddy while he smiled back at me. When he finally finished working the gel onto each strain of hair, my head was as greasy as a quart of Pennzoil.

I grew up in the tiny town of Washington Park, North Carolina, which is nestled on the Pamlico River and has a population of around five hundred. On Sunday mornings, most houses in Washington Park were bustling with families getting ready for church, and the Bowen home was no exception. My parents, my older brother, Lee, and I lived in a small ranch-style house with three bedrooms and one bathroom. That image of my dad grooming my hair before church triggered another memory for me: this one of me and Lee sitting beside my grandmother in her self-reserved church pew. Gramma, as we affectionately called her, was a pillar at First Christian Church. She was also an active member of the Christian Women's Fellowship, a devout group of women who formed the backbone of the church in the 1950s and '60s. They organized bazaars and collected trading stamps and used clothing to provide for those less fortunate. When racial tensions were high in the community, these willful women pushed our minister, Dr. Alexander, to endorse a Christian attitude toward racial integration, and he listened. For years, he preached from his pulpit that racial bigotry and intolerance had no place in the Christian faith.

During this particular flashback, as I sat next to Gramma in church, Dr. Alexander called for the members of the congregation to bow their heads for the benediction. I watched as my grandmother closed her bright blue eyes and grabbed my hand as well

CHAPTER 1

as my brother's. After the brief prayer, she continued whispering to herself. When she finished, I asked, "Gramma, why did you grab my hand?"

"Because I wanted you to feel the love of Jesus," she said.

Still lying helpless in my Baja Bug, this memory of my grandmother fades as consciousness resurfaces. Waking from the memory of my grandmother, I mutter a prayer to God, pleading for him to please take me away from here.

As Dr. Hatcher continues to reassure me that an ambulance is on the way, I wonder, *What are the chances that one of my professors would be here comforting me at this vulnerable moment in my life?* Dr. Hatcher and I befriended each other a year earlier when he found out I was on the university's tennis team. An avid player himself, he occasionally talked to me about tennis after class.

In another moment of lucidity, I remember what I'm wearing. I panic, thinking that the paramedics will treat me differently if they think I'm a transvestite. But again, a sense of calm pervades as I fall unconscious. The viewfinder reveals two images of me during my childhood that assure me I can withstand any embarrassment, even that resulting from my current attire.

In one image, I'm standing on the side of the street in front of our house. I appear to be around six years old. The image is so lifelike that it seems like I could reach out my hand, grab this little boy, and pull him away from the road to keep him from embarrassing himself. I see myself frantically trying to get my belt unbuckled while holding a football tucked underneath my arm.

It was late fall, and I'd been playing football by myself in the front yard. I was

THE VIEWFINDER

dressed in the Washington Redskins football uniform Mama had ordered for me from the Sears catalog. At this stage in my life, I had developed quite a strange habit. Whenever I heard a car coming down our street, I would dash to the side of the road, quickly pull down my pants, and eagerly await the passing car. As the car approached, I would sing my made-up song: "Ring daddy ring daddy ring-ring-ring, what-a-ya know, pull down your pants, pee on the car!"

On this particular day, my neighbor Mrs. Buckman was the lucky loser at the wheel when I attempted to spray her car. But as hard as I tried to pee on her car, I just didn't have the power in my stream. She immediately pulled over, got out of the car, and yelled my name. I quickly dropped the football and pulled up my pants as I ran into the house. The knock on the kitchen door came just as I made it to my bedroom. I could hear the muffled conversation between my mom and Mrs. Buckman. A few minutes later, my mom called me into the kitchen, where I received a spanking and the proverbial words of warning: "Michael Jarvis Bowen, there is a direct relationship between your head and your heinie. When your head causes you to do things you shouldn't do, your heinie is going to pay the price."

When I was growing up, my parents believed spankings were a necessary deterrent against doing the wrong thing, and they were to a certain extent. However, sometimes the promise of pleasure outweighed the risk of a spanking. For me, the forbidden fruit was the banana bike of my brother's friend Charlie.

The next image the viewfinder reveals is me looking out the screen door of the kitchen, staring at the familiar faces of John, Tommy, and Charlie who also

CHAPTER 1

live in Washington Park. Me and Lee were part of a close-knit group of eleven neighborhood kids, known as the Park Boys, who shared similar interests such as riding bicycles.

John, Tommy, and Charlie were closer in age to Lee, who is three and a half years older than me, so I always felt special getting to hang out with them. One night, shortly after my seventh birthday, they invited me to go for a bike ride after dinner. To my surprise, Charlie even offered to let me ride his bike. For weeks, I'd been admiring his gold metal flake bike with its leopard skin seat and high sissy bar. But whenever I asked if I could ride it, the answer was always no. So when he offered to let me ride his bike, I was ecstatic. But as soon as I walked to the end of the driveway and mounted the bike, Tommy grabbed me by the shirt and said, while trying his best to keep a straight face, "If you're gonna ride Charlie's bike, you gotta ride it naked." Eager to get on the road, I stripped down to my birthday suit without hesitation.

Charlie and John were laughing, so I started laughing too, even though I didn't know what we were laughing about. While I knew it was wrong to pull down my pants and pee on cars, I didn't see the harm in riding around the block naked, especially if I was riding Charlie's bike. So I hopped on that banana bike and away I went, naked as a jaybird with my entourage in tow. Charlie, who was riding Lee's bike, kept reminding me not to sit down on his seat. The seat was too high for me anyway, so I pedaled standing up as a feeling of euphoria washed over me. Now and then, I looked over my shoulder at the three of them, and their cheers of encouragement put an even bigger smile on my face.

As I headed down our street, I saw John's mom sweeping the sidewalk in front of her house. John called out, "Hey, Mom, look at Michael!" Somewhat startled to hear her son's voice, Mrs. Robinson looked up, waved, then smiled, and continued to sweep.

"Oh my God!" Tommy shouted. "She didn't even notice!"

Although Mrs. Robinson didn't realize I was streaking, Mrs. Buckman across the street sure did!

The first phone call to my house came in around six thirty. "Hi, Betty. It's Melanie. I . . . uh . . . wanted to let you know that Michael just passed by our house riding a bicycle without a stitch of clothing on."

I turned onto Spruce Street and went by the Fulcher house. No sooner had Mama hung up with Mrs. Buckman when the phone rang again. "Hello, Betty. It's Naomi Fulcher. Your youngest one—"

"I know," my mom interrupted her with a laugh. "He's naked again. I just got a call from Melanie, who saw him go by her house. I'm going to go get him now."

I was in the home stretch and had just made it back around the block to Fairview Avenue when I saw Mama standing at the end of our driveway with her hands planted firmly on her hips. Like most children, I wanted to impress my mom since I was riding a "big boy" bike. So I sat my rear end on the crossbar of the bike—much to Charlie's chagrin—let go of the handlebars and jubilantly whooped, "Look, Mama, no hands!"

CHAPTER 1

"And no clothes either," my mom retorted. "Get off that bicycle and get in this house *now!*"

The sound of a distant siren pulls me back to reality. Although the glass in my eyes causes tremendous pain, I open one eye to see my body still languishing in the passenger seat. I clear my head and briefly smile, thankful to be lying in this mangled car fully dressed and not stark naked. Although I'm no longer frantic about the outfit I'm wearing, I feel compelled to explain to Dr. Hatcher why I'm dressed this way. I try to take a deep breath but stop short when I feel a piercing pain in my rib cage.

Persevering through the pain, I mumble to my professor through gritted teeth, "Dr. Hatcher, this is a costume. I was an extra in a movie downtown." I don't know if he can hear or understand me, but he continues to tell me that help is on the way.

My parents are going to be so disappointed when they hear I've been in an accident. I caused them so much anguish growing up. Peeing on cars and riding naked around the block was just the tip of the iceberg. With my eyes closed, I see image after image of my impish past through the lens of the viewfinder.

In one image, I'm sitting in the truck of J. T. Harris, a close family friend, after running away from home at age five. Actually, I pedaled away on my red Radio Flyer tricycle. Tired of trekking up and down Fairview Avenue, I asked Mama if I could ride around the block. But she said, "Absolutely not!" I didn't really want to ride around the block. I just wanted to spread my wings and venture up to Clover Farm Country Store, which was several blocks away, so I did.

THE VIEWFINDER

Clover Farm was near the park, and in order to get there, you had to cross River Road, a busy two-lane highway. When I arrived at the store, I parked my tricycle out front, went inside, and grabbed a Dr. Pepper and a pack of Sugar Babies. At the checkout counter, I stood on my tippy-toes and put my drink, candy, and a quarter on the counter. But Mrs. Daisy, the store manager, informed me that I was ten cents short. When I told her that was all the money I had, she smiled and put my drink and candy in a small brown paper bag.

Once outside, I could hear dirt bikes revving their engines behind the store, so I followed the noise until I saw two guys riding up and down large mounds of sawdust and making huge rooster tails. A little further away, several kids were standing on the railroad tracks picking up rocks and seeing who could throw them the farthest. It looked like fun, and I was good at throwing rocks.

To get to the railroad tracks, you had to travel a short distance down Brick Kiln Road. As I pedaled toward the tracks, the feelings of independence, adventure, and mischief were all wrapped up in one big ear-to-ear grin. I had just reached the tracks when J. T. Harris stopped, backed up, got out of his truck, and asked, "Michael, son, pray tell, what are you doin' near these train tracks?"

"I'm gonna throw some rocks," I answered rather excitedly.

"Let's put your tricycle in the back of my truck and go talk to your daddy first," he suggested.

"No!" I stubbornly replied. "I'm gonna stay and throw some rocks with my friends."

CHAPTER 1

"Son, I'm takin' you home, so go get in the truck," Mr. Harris ordered.

Mr. Harris was ruffling the feathers of my independence, and I didn't like it. So with lightning speed, I picked up a rock and flung it at him. And also with lightning speed, I was in his truck, bawling my eyes out. He drove me home and explained to my mom where he'd found me. By this time, she was frantic. She'd already called the neighbors and Daddy, who was on his way home from work.

I knew I was going to get a spanking—maybe even a whipping! You might wonder, *What's the difference?* Well, in the Bowen household, a spanking involved the use of a bare hand; a whipping required the use of a switch. Much to my surprise, I didn't receive either. Instead, my parents sat me down and explained the dangers of going near the railroad tracks. It was one of the few times I ever saw Mama and Daddy cry.

In another image that passes through the lens of the viewfinder, I am seven years old and have a water hose in one hand and the screen door to the kitchen in the other. I had just finished pedaling up and down Bank Street with Bill Batchelor, my friend who lived behind us. We'd been dodging imaginary firebombs and machine-gun blasts as we rode our bikes into a barricade of leaves. When I returned home, I noticed that these death-defying acts had made for a dirty bicycle. Unsatisfied with the job the garage rags were doing to clean my bike, I decided our new electric toothbrush would be just the thing to restore the metallic blue shine on my bike. As I was finishing up, Aunt Bessy saw what I was up to when she came to the kitchen door to call me in for lunch.

"Child, what are you doin'. Give me that toothbrush!" she demanded, her voice full of disgust. She yanked the toothbrush from my hand, and then with her other hand, she jerked me up on my feet and gave me two swift smacks across my rear. "I should call your daddy right now and tell him what you've done. Don't you touch that toothbrush again, you hear me?"

Unbeknownst to me, Aunt Bessy wasn't my aunt. She was a stocky, proud Black woman, who looked after Lee and me sometimes during the summer months while our parents were at work. Aunt Bessy treated my brother and me like we were her children and administered an equal amount of affection or tough love as needed. She had Mama and Daddy's blessing to discipline us for inappropriate behavior, but immediately following the slaps across my fanny, I gave her a piece of my mind. However, before I could get two words out of my mouth, she gave me another swat across my bottom and went back inside the house, electric toothbrush in hand.

As the initial pain from the spanking wore off, I reasoned that I shouldn't get a spanking just for cleaning my bicycle, so I decided I was going to teach Aunt Bessy a lesson. I looked down and noticed the water hose on the ground next to my bike. Glancing through the screen door, I could see Aunt Bessy putting lunch on the kitchen table. I stealthily grabbed the water hose and slowly opened the door, then I took aim, squeezed the nozzle, and bull's-eye—I squirted Aunt Bessy squarely in the back! When the water hit her in the derriere, she let out a high-pitched squeal, and my bologna sandwich and potato chips went flying through the air. Aunt Bessy ran out of the kitchen to escape my revenge, but I continued

CHAPTER 1

to let her have it until she was no longer in range. Once she was out of sight, I dropped the water hose and ran behind the house to hide, but I could hear her screaming my name.

"Michael Bowen, you are a devil child! The devil is in you! You wait 'til your daddy gets home!" she roared.

Maybe Aunt Bessy was right. Perhaps the devil was in me. As a kid, all I did was get in trouble and cause my parents grief. In Sunday school, they taught us to obey our parents because it pleased God. But it didn't matter that I attended Sunday school, Bible school, or church because I wasn't applying any of the lessons I learned. If obeying your parents pleased God, seeing me steal ice-cream sandwiches from the school cafeteria surely displeased him.

In the next image I click in the viewfinder, I'm standing in the lunch line holding a plastic tray full of food. My friends, Rusty and Kyle are a few places behind me, jockeying to get a view of my first heist. I'm excited but nervous. A day earlier, during sixth grade recess, I overheard a few boys bragging about how easy it was to steal ice-cream sandwiches from the cafeteria. "You just grab the ice-cream sandwich, slip it under your tray with one hand, and give your lunch ticket to the cashier with the other," one of them said.

As I neared the freezer bin, I noticed a cafeteria staff member bringing out a fresh box of ice-cream sandwiches. She opened the box but left it on top of the freezer. As I approached the bin, she removed the empty box and walked away with it. So I reached up, grabbed the fresh box, and placed it into the freezer. After

THE VIEWFINDER

making sure the coast was clear, I reached into the bin, nonchalantly grabbed a milk, then quickly retrieved an ice-cream sandwich and placed it underneath my tray. Finally, I turned and gave my lunch ticket to the cashier. She looked at my tray, then at me, paused, and said, "Young man, do you owe me any more money?"

"No ma'am," I responded with as much confidence as I could muster.

"Are you sure?" she asked.

"Yes ma'am," I replied.

"Okay, go have a seat," she said, shaking her head as I turned toward the tables.

As I walked away, I felt something brushing against my pant leg. I glanced down and saw that the ice-cream sandwich I intended to steal had four more attached to it! Panic-stricken, I briskly walked to my seat while trying to gather the tangled string of evidence into my hand. But while corralling the ice-cream sandwiches, my carton of milk toppled off my tray, which drew the attention and laughter of several students. So I quickly picked up my milk and rushed to my seat with the ice-cream sandwiches still bouncing off my leg.

After sitting down, I nervously looked behind me at the cashier. She was taking someone else's lunch ticket, so I thought maybe she hadn't seen what I'd done. Perhaps I had a little too much food on my tray and that was why she'd asked me if I owed more money. Nevertheless, I thought it would be a good idea to get rid of the evidence, so I gave the four extra ice-cream sandwiches away and started eating the one I'd intended to steal. While I scarfed down my dessert, I continued to glance over my shoulder at the cashier. I had about half of the ice-cream

CHAPTER 1

sandwich crammed into my mouth when I felt a tap on my shoulder. Looking up, I saw Mrs. Jackson, the cafeteria manager, and the cashier standing behind me.

"Mrs. Howard, is this the young man who stole the ice-cream sandwiches?" Mrs. Jackson asked.

"Yes, he's the one," Mrs. Howard responded confidently.

"Aren't you Bo Bowen's son?" Mrs. Jackson asked.

"Yes, ma'am," I muttered, gagging on the mouthful of evidence I'd just swallowed.

"Doesn't your daddy work over at the ABC Store?" she inquired, looking around the lunch table at the other saucer-eyed students.

"Yes ma'am," I acknowledged, nodding my head.

Mrs. Jackson squatted down and leaned in so her face was right next to my ear. Loud enough for the students at my table to hear, she said, "You finish the ice-cream sandwich you have crammed into your mouth, but I'll be givin' your daddy a call today."

Mrs. Jackson stood up, turned around, and walked away from the table. The boys sitting near me just stared, waiting for me to say something. I nervously giggled at my mishap, but I knew Daddy was going to kill me.

Bewildered, Rusty asked, "Why did you steal *five* ice-cream sandwiches?"

"I only meant to steal one!" I answered.

One boy at the table had the answer to my debacle. He explained that the cafeteria workers leave the fresh box of ice-cream sandwiches on top of the freezer

THE VIEWFINDER

until they can pull them apart. Then they place them in the bin.

As the guys at the table laughed at me, I tried to play it cool and laughed along with them, even though I was on the verge of tears. When lunch was over, I rushed to the bathroom. Unable to hold in the tears any longer, I started crying. I glanced into the mirror at my reflection, and for the first time in my life, I felt ashamed. I had disappointed my mother and father yet again.

I spent the rest of the school day worried about what I was going to say to my parents. When three thirty finally arrived, I raced out of school and jumped on my bike. All the way home, I anxiously weighed my options: 1) don't go home at all, just run away; 2) wreck my bicycle and hope Mama and Daddy feel so bad about my injuries that they ignore my thievery; 3) maybe, just maybe, Mrs. Jackson will forget to call my father. He only worked a few miles away from the school, so surely if she'd called him at work, he would've immediately left and come to the school.

As I pedaled into the driveway, I noticed Daddy wasn't home from work yet, so I took that as a positive sign. Getting off my bike, I told myself to play it cool. I walked into the house as I did every day, calmly made my way to my bedroom, and tossed my book bag on the floor. In passing, Mama asked how my day was. I told her it was fine. Then I headed to the refrigerator for some milk and grabbed a few cookies from the pantry. As I sat down at the kitchen table to eat my snack, Mama came into the kitchen.

"What are you doin'?" she asked in a perplexed tone of voice.

"Just havin' some milk and cookies," I replied.

CHAPTER 1

"How could you *possibly* be hungry after eating all those ice-cream sandwiches you stole at lunch today?" she snapped. I instantly felt light-headed and sick to my stomach. "Put the milk and cookies down, go to your room, and stay there until your daddy gets home!"

I tried to explain what had happened, but my mom had no interest in my account of the incident.

Spending two hours in my room waiting for my father might as well have been two hours in solitary confinement. My room was a place to sleep, and this was torture! I had no television, no phone, and no radio, only a bed and a set of 1966 *World Book* encyclopedias. To me, two hours of this should've been punishment enough.

Daddy walked through the door around six thirty. I could hear Mama talking to him in the kitchen, but I couldn't make out what they were saying. A few minutes later, Daddy called from the hallway, "Michael, come have a seat in the living room."

When the two of them walked into the living room, Mama sat down across from me. Daddy, however, stood in the middle of the room with his hands on his hips and stared right at me. I met his gaze but only for a second before hanging my head.

Daddy got right to the point saying, "Son, why did you steal those ice-cream sandwiches today?"

"Because my friends dared me to," I mumbled nervously, but that was a lie. I'd stolen the ice-cream sandwiches to see if I could get away with it. Even so, I was telling the truth when I said that I thought stealing them made me look cool in front of my friends.

Daddy looked at me and calmly said, "If you need to steal things to impress your friends, then you need new friends. Genuine friends don't encourage you to do the wrong thing. Son, look at me and listen carefully. Now that you've stolen something, adults around you may not trust you anymore. People who steal from others also lie to others and cheat others. It hurts my heart to know your mother and I have raised a son who people cannot trust. Some people may think that because I'm your father, I'm not trustworthy either."

Daddy didn't have to raise his voice to get his point across. His soft-spoken words were gut-wrenching and shook me to the core. I was a thief, a liar, and a cheat. I wept uncontrollably as both of them continued to explain how disappointed they were in me. My parents told me to take a walk around the block and pull myself together while they decided on an appropriate punishment for my actions. As I walked, I thought about what my parents had said and what Gramma would think of my actions. As a God-fearing woman, my grandmother had no tolerance for those who stole from others. If she knew her grandson was a thief, she would've reminded me of the commandment, "You shall not steal." Gramma had no tolerance for those who commit besetting sins.

When I returned from my walk and learned my punishment, I realized Daddy believed stealing was a serious offense. To pay back the cafeteria for the five ice-cream sandwiches I'd stolen, I worked there in the mornings before school and during recess

CHAPTER 1

for a week. On Friday afternoon, Daddy and I walked into the cafeteria where I paid Mrs. Jackson fifty cents for the ice-cream sandwiches and apologized for my actions. After that, I never stole another ice-cream sandwich—or anything—ever again.

Daddy was right about the impact my actions had on my reputation. As the news of my theft spread around school, several of my favorite teachers told me how disappointed they were in me, and they hoped I could repair my good name. Although Daddy never stopped loving me, he stopped liking me for a while after that incident.

The sound of Dr. Hatcher's voice penetrates my subconscious and stops the images I see. "Michael, the paramedics are here. You're going to be okay," he assures.

Moments later, I hear another voice. "Hey, Mr. Bowen, we're EMTs here to help you."

Before they can say another word, I feel the need to explain my attire to them. "I'm not a transvestite. I was in a Schwarzenegger movie!" There's no reply to my statement, so I continue, "I'm a tennis player at—"

"What's your name?" a paramedic asks.

"Michael," I respond.

"Michael, my name is Alex. This is Kaleb. We're here to help you, but it's important that you try not to move."

Once more, I attempt to open my eyes, but the pain is excruciating. "I can't open my eyes. There's glass in my eyes!" I sputter as a mixture of blood and saliva spew out of my mouth.

The paramedics say nothing and begin assessing my injuries. As they throw medical jargon back and forth, I'm relieved to know that I'm in excellent hands.

The next thing I remember is the bumpy ride to the hospital jarring me awake. I have no memory of being removed from my car and put into the ambulance. On the way to the hospital, Alex asks if there's someone he can contact to let them know I've been in a car accident. I tell him to call my roommate. I complain again to the paramedic that I have broken glass in my eyes. Alex tells me to keep my eyes closed. That's easy for him to say, but I can't. I have to see what's going on around me. I fight through the pain to open one eye and see that my forehead is secured with first aid tape. I also feel a brace around my neck. Kaleb seems to be getting every bit of horsepower out of the rig's engine, and the quick stops and starts are causing equipment to clang around me. As I listen to these sounds, I cannot believe what's happening. *Why did I agree to dress up in this stupid outfit and stand around all day for nothing? I just want to turn back time.*

CHAPTER 2

ONE NURSE IS cutting off the T-shirt and jean jacket I'm wearing while two other nurses are taking off my tights, shoes, socks, and costume accessories. A fourth nurse tends to the cuts on my face and arms. It's controlled chaos in the emergency room. I hear multiple conversations from doctors and nurses all at once. One question after another is being fired at me.

"Mr. Bowen, I'm Dr. Sheldon. Can you tell me your full name?"

"Michael Jarvis Bowen," I respond.

"Mr. Bowen, how old are you?"

"Twenty-three."

"Very good, and do you take any medications?"

"No."

"Have you had any alcohol today?"

"No."

"Mr. Bowen, can you feel me touching you?"

"No."

"How about now?"

"No."

"How about now?"

"No! I can't feel anything but my face!" I answer, panic-stricken.

"Mr. Bowen, can you feel me touching your neck?"

"Yes."

"Is the feeling sharp or dull?"

"Sharp."

"Positive for Babinski reflex and moderate clonus in the right ankle," a voice says.

I want the questions to stop long enough for me to explain why I have on mascara, why I'm dressed this way. Someone in the room explains that I was an extra in a movie, which puts my mind at ease.

"Can someone please get the glass out of my eyes?" I plead.

A few seconds later, someone opens each of my eyes and drenches the insides with a watery solution. Once. Twice. Three times this solution fills each eye.

The medical lingo continues to swirl around me as Dr. Sheldon barks out commands. "Let's get X-rays of his cervical and lumbar spine and an ultrasound of his abdomen."

As the doctor continues requesting tests, I look up and the ER lights spin. The next thing I know, I'm lying facedown on a stretcher that resembles an old military cot with a small opening for my face. The tile flooring beneath me is so

CHAPTER 2

shiny it looks wet. I'm confused because moments earlier, I was lying on my back with doctors and nurses poking and prodding me. Now it's quiet, and I can only hear a few voices off in the distance. Soon, I hear footsteps and the sound of a curtain being opened as the room gets brighter.

"Hey, Michael. My name's Jamie. I'm one of the ER nurses here."

"Where am I?"

"You're still in the emergency room at New Hanover Regional Medical Center," she adds.

"Why am I lying facedown?"

"You're on a Stryker frame bed," she replies. She later explains that this contraption is sandwiching me between two metal frameworks covered with canvas, which allows me to be rotated 360 degrees in order to keep my lungs clear and prevent pressure sores while stabilizing my head and neck. For a claustrophobic person, this is not the place to be.

As I stare down at the floor, I muster up the courage to ask Jamie one more question before she leaves. "How long do I have to stay like this?"

"About an hour and a half, then we'll turn you on your back," she responds.

"No, I mean, when can I get out of this contraption?"

"Sweetheart, I don't know. That's up to the doctors," she says in a comforting voice. "I do know that your parents have been contacted, and they're on their way to Wilmington."

Time slowly creeps by, and I'm left alone with my thoughts. I try to think of other challenging experiences from my past to bring me some small level of solace, but my mind is swirling with other thoughts. *Is my neck broken? Why else am I not able to move or feel anything below my neck? I mean, people die from broken necks. Am I going to die?*

I close my eyes and silently pray: *God, please don't let me die! I'm not ready!* I pray this desperate prayer several times, then I think to myself, *What a rookie prayer. Who am I to tell God if I'm ready to die or not? My prayer should be, Please don't let me die yet; I'm not sure if I'm going to heaven!*

The thought of death overwhelms me, so I close my eyes and search my mind for other thoughts. A conversation I had with my grandmother comes to mind. We were sitting on her beloved porch swing overlooking the Pamlico River. I was young, but I knew how to read. Inside her cross-stitch basket, which sat on a small table beside her, was Billy Graham's book *Angels: God's Secret Agents*.

I asked, "Gramma, do you believe in angels?"

"I certainly do," she said. "In fact, you were named after an angel." I watched her eyes widen as she told me with certainty, "The Bible tells us we all have a guardian angel that looks out for us."

"Who is my guardian angel?" I asked.

"I don't know, but you'll know when the time is right," she assured.

After reliving that conversation with my grandmother, I think to myself, *Was my guardian angel with me while I lay helpless in my car today? Was my guardian angel providing me with those vivid images from my childhood to distract me from*

CHAPTER 2

the painful reality facing me? Why don't I remember being pulled out of my car? Was that my guardian angel's way of keeping me calm?

When a curtain opens, thoughts of my guardian angel stop. Two nurses enter the room, and I recognize Jamie's voice. The other nurse introduces herself as Phyllis. Jamie tells me they're going to rotate me onto my back. It's a slow process.

As soon as I'm flat on my back, I feel nauseous. I tell Jamie that I'm sick to my stomach, and just as she and Phyllis rotate me onto my side, vomit mixed with blood erupts from my mouth, saturating the shiny floor below. Jamie works quickly to retrieve a bedpan and just as she gets it under my mouth, I vomit again, peppering the pan and most of her sleeve. They turn me facedown as I continue to dry heave. Lying on my stomach, I feel as though my eyes are being pulled out of their sockets by the sheer force of gravity.

Feeling sorry for myself with my vulnerability exposed, I watch as tears drip from the tip of my nose into the smelly cocktail below. Jamie and Phyllis roll my bed away from the vomitus stench. I try, unsuccessfully, to hold my breath so I don't make any noise as I cry.

While they clean up my mess, I apologize profusely to Jamie for throwing up on her. She assures me that it's no big deal. After sanitizing the floor, they slowly turn me on my side. Jamie kneels so she's at my eye level and shows me a small cup with a pill in it. She says it'll help calm the nausea. I glance at the pill and then at her. She's not much older than I am. Her kind eyes and gentle voice convey the deep compassion required to be an excellent nurse. I take the medicine and remain on my side as the nausea subsides.

Ten minutes later, Jamie and Phyllis return to the room. Jamie leans over me and says, "Michael, there's a lady in the waiting room who claims to be your mother, and she's demanding to see you."

"What? I'm confused. Why would my mom be here without my dad?" I ask.

"I don't know, but there's a Mrs. Bowen in the waiting room who insists on seeing her son," Jamie clarifies.

Phyllis states that the woman is hysterical, and hospital security is restraining her. They want to roll my bed near the waiting room entrance so I can verify whether or not the woman is actually my mother. Jamie and Phyllis rotate me onto my back, unlock the wheels to my bed, and start rolling me down the short hallway to the emergency room doors. I can tell the Stryker frame is heavy as the two of them struggle to navigate it down the hallway.

When we reach the entrance, they rotate the bed so I am on my side and can see through the door. I can hear a woman intermittently crying and arguing with the security guards restraining her. As the doors open automatically, I look straight ahead and make eye contact with the woman. She sees me and instantly stops squirming. For a second, her face is vacant of emotion. Then she slightly smiles and says with relief in her voice, "That's not my son! He's not my son."

Phyllis hits the button to close the doors. Upset, she and Jamie apologize to me for having put me through this uncomfortable ordeal. Together, they rotate my bed so I'm facing up then roll me back to my curtained room. Lying there with

CHAPTER 2

my eyes closed, I keep seeing the panic leave that lady's face when she realized that I wasn't her son. *My parents won't be so lucky,* I think to myself.

Reality retreats from my mind, and reluctantly, my thoughts return to dying. I ponder the question: *If I die, am I going to heaven? Does anyone truly know that when they die? Do they know with absolute certainty that they're going to heaven?* These thoughts remind me of a Sunday school class from childhood where we sat and colored pictures of heaven. I remember coloring the pearly gates, two angels flying above them, and a winding road ascending into the clouds. After we finished coloring our pictures, we gathered around for the lesson. The Sunday school teacher told us before we entered heaven through the pearly gates, God would show us a book that listed all the deeds—both good and evil—that we'd committed here on earth. She said it was important to always love your parents, brothers, and sisters and to be kind to everyone, including strangers.

Confined to this bed, I keep hearing the teacher say, "be kind to everyone," over and over in my head. As if I'm a puppet and God is the puppet master, he maneuvers my mind through two memories while I sleep. These memories are shameful, and I don't want to relive them, but I'm powerless to stop them.

Thankfully, wicked deeds do not prevent you from entering heaven's pearly gates because if they do, I'm surely going to hell—but not because I peed on my neighbor's car or squirted Aunt Bessy with the water hose. No, I'm going to hell because I was unkind, even cruel, to Trey and Annie.

While trapped inside the Stryker frame, I see an image of William, one of the meanest kids in school, pinning Trey into the corner of Mrs. Wynne's classroom. I was making my way into eighth-grade typing class when I witnessed the incident. The two boys were nose to nose with each other. Trey, who was scared of William, moved his upper body vigorously back and forth, which was a symptom of his autism. But watching Trey jerk backward and forward freaked William out. He didn't want to hurt Trey; he just wanted information that only Trey could provide.

Trey was a gentle giant. He stood six feet tall, weighed over two hundred pounds, and had bushy blond hair that reminded me of the Cowardly Lion from *The Wizard of Oz*. Trey also had a special gift: he was a "calendar kid." You could tell Trey your date of birth, and he had the uncanny ability to tell you what day of the week you were born, regardless of your age. It didn't matter if you were born in 1975 or 1875. And on this day, William wanted to know what day of the week he was born on; Trey just wanted to make his way to his desk.

Like William and others, I liked to harass Trey, often referring to him as "Retard." I would force him to recall the day I was born and the birthdays of famous people. If he didn't provide this information to me on demand, I would raise my voice and threaten him until he did. But William picked the wrong day to back Trey into a corner—figuratively and literally. When Trey refused to tell him the day of his birth, William pushed him up against the wall. Trey panicked, screamed, and shoved William backward so he could run away. But Trey's unbridled strength sent William to the floor like a rag doll. To add insult to injury, Trey stomped on William's chest as he ran out of the classroom.

CHAPTER 2

Reliving this childhood memory, I feel so ashamed. Although it was William who ended up on the nasty floor, my hands were dirty too. Just like William, I picked on Trey as a form of entertainment. Out of all the students in the school I could harass, I chose someone with autism. But why? Why be cruel to anyone? I don't know why I did it. I only know there's a reason I'm reliving this memory: God is teaching me a lesson about compassion toward others who are different from me. As I remember this incident, the empathy I feel for Trey is palpable. I want to talk some sense into my teenage self, but you don't get do-overs.

Shortly after recalling the unkind memory of how Trey was treated, I see Annie sitting in the back of Mr. Hodges's North Carolina History class in seventh grade, her eyes focused on me. Oh, how I do not want to relive this memory, but my mind won't focus on anything else.

Mr. Hodges was my favorite teacher. He made the history of North Carolina come alive. But it didn't stop me from picking on Annie when I got the chance. Like Trey, Annie was also autistic. She was tall and frail, and her face was riddled with acne most of the time. She wore thick, outdated, black-framed glasses and a single barrette to hold her oily, black, shoulder-length hair in place. Most days, she wore a cardigan sweater and khaki pants that were too short for her long legs. And she carried her textbooks, which were covered in brown paper grocery bags and labeled by academic subject, in a large canvas bag. Annie was an oddity, so most students left her alone.

She spoke in a robotic voice and was not very social. At age twelve, I was

THE VIEWFINDER

self-absorbed and ignorant and thought Annie was dumb. However, her teachers knew firsthand that she was not only intelligent but also talented. And unbeknownst to me or my friends, Annie had a beautiful singing voice. Her nasally speech transformed into lovely music when she opened her mouth to sing.

Annie also had two odd fixations that I exploited at opportune times. The first was that she hated it when students clicked their tongues. Like a few other jerks, I was guilty of clicking my tongue whenever I saw her in the hallways. Another oddity was her love of books—but not just the pleasure of *reading* books, Annie felt the need to take care of them. Her teachers knew about this passion and purposefully seated her near the supplemental books in each of her classes. She was always assigned as the overseer of these books and took great pride in passing them out and picking them up at the end of class. Understandably, Annie's stress level climbed sharply when students used these books. And experience told her that Michael Bowen would harm one of her beloved books if he got the chance.

In this memory, Mr. Hodges asked Annie to pass out the supplementary history books for our assigned reading. Annie rarely read during this time because she was on alert for anyone who might harm one of her precious books. Some students teased Annie, but I was probably the cruelest.

Shortly after Annie finished passing out the books and returned to her seat, I began hyperextending my book's cover. When Annie heard the distress call of glue pulling away from the spine and the pages of the book, she jumped up from her desk and rushed over to me.

CHAPTER 2

"Give me that book, Michael Bowen!" she said angrily.

"No! Go away," I grumbled through clenched teeth.

Annie reached for the book, but I quickly snatched it out of her hands. Agitated, she turned abruptly and walked rapidly to Mr. Hodges's desk in a huff. "Mr. Hodges, Michael Bowen is hurting that history book," she accused as she pointed at me and wagged her finger.

Mr. Hodges looked over at me with disappointment. I just smiled and mumbled under my breath that I was sorry.

But I wasn't sorry. At the end of class when Annie was collecting the books, I got out a clean piece of paper, put it inside my history book, and tore the paper. Annie thought I was tearing a page from the book. Distraught, she ran over to my desk and tried unsuccessfully to pry the book from my hands. She glanced over at Mr. Hodges's desk, only to realize that he was in the hallway. Torn between leaving me with the book or venturing into the hallway to complain to Mr. Hodges, Annie stayed with the book and begged me to give it to her. As soon as I did, she frantically thumbed through the book, trying to find the torn page. I left the class with my friends in tow, chuckling over my mistreatment of Annie. That day, I enjoyed the attention of my friends. When you suffer from chronic low self-esteem, sometimes negative attention is better than no attention at all. It's pathetic, but it's true.

As I'm jostled from this memory, I'm disgusted with myself. If I could punch my younger self in the face, I would. *I deserve to be lying in this godforsaken contraption,* I think. *Aunt Bessy was right, the devil is in me!*

THE VIEWFINDER

In the emergency room, time is hard to measure. I don't know if the images, thoughts, and memories go on for seconds, minutes, or hours. Sometime after the hysterical woman realized I was not her son, my parents arrive. When they enter my room, I'm lying facedown, so I'm unable to see them.

The first words out of my mouth are to my father, "Daddy, I really messed up this time."

He kneels down to comfort me and replies, "Your Mama and I are here now, so you just rest." I've never been so relieved to hear my daddy's voice.

Not long after my parents arrive, Dr. Sheldon and Jamie come in. The doctor introduces himself to my parents, but there's no small talk between them. He informs me and my parents that initial tests and CAT scans confirm that I have a contused spinal cord injury and a pedicle fracture of my fourth cervical vertebra, which are causing paralysis from the neck down. After delivering this shocking news, he turns and quickly disappears through the curtain.

Hearing Dr. Sheldon say "paralysis from the neck down" petrifies me. A small part of me wants to ask him if I'll ever walk again. But a much larger part of me doesn't want to know.

Jamie remains in the room, and I hear her whisper to my parents, "I'm so sorry." Then she kneels down under the bed, meets my gaze with sympathetic eyes, and says, "I'm right outside the curtain if you need me, okay."

Mama leans down and tells me she and Daddy are going to step out of the room for a few minutes. I'm emotionally drained and want to scream, "Someone

CHAPTER 2

get me out of this goddamn torture chamber!" but I'm too tired. I don't have the strength to yell. I want to muscle my way out of this metal hellhole, but all I can do is blink my eyes. As a depth of despair I've never experienced before washes over me, I think to myself, *What sort of sadist builds a machine like this?*

Again, I plead with God, *Please take me away from here. Let me fall asleep and dream of happier times. Let me escape my tears, the blood, and the vomit.* I'm like a frightened child who is scared of the unknown. I wish someone could just calm this fear inside me. I detest this feeling—this weakness. I think of my younger cousin Jonathan, who's only nine years old. He was born with a rare congenital heart defect that's required him to spend most of his life at Duke Children's Hospital. *Why can't I be brave like him?*

With my parents out of the room, I watch as tears slowly drip off the bridge of my nose and hit the floor. *If there's a hell on earth, I'm in it.* When they return, Daddy tells me two of my teammates are in the waiting room and would like to see me. When Jamie comes in to check on me, Daddy asks if two of my friends can visit.

"Are these teammates like family?" she asks, baiting Daddy to say yes.

"They are tonight," he responds.

Before I can say no, that I don't want my teammates to see me like this, Jamie tells my parents I can only have two visitors at a time, so they need to follow her to the waiting room and she'll escort my teammates back to see me. A few minutes later, Kermit and Rock walk in.

They make chitchat while lying on the floor beneath me, but I can tell that they're uncomfortable being here. It takes a lot of courage to confront your worst fear as a college athlete: being paralyzed. They try to cheer me up with humor, which is the best way they know how.

On the UNC–Wilmington tennis team, no one escapes being teased. We usually exploit each other's physical flaws or fabricate one if we can't find one. I have two nicknames: "Vienna" and "Sifter," the first due to my short, sausage-like fingers and the second thanks to a gap between my front teeth. Kermit, who dubbed me Sifter, enjoys making fun of me whenever the tennis team goes out to dinner. Occasionally, he'll wave over the server with his fingers bent, mimicking my stubby digits. When the server arrives at our table, Kermit will ask for a toothpick for himself and a broomstick for me. His antics always get a laugh from everyone, including me. I know it's all in good fun.

Now Kermit is lying on the floor, smiling up at me, and waving his abbreviated hand. I'm not sure how much they know about my condition, but, like true teammates, they tell me, "Bowen, you got this, man. You're in the best shape of anybody on the team. You're going to make a full recovery, brother."

They've only been there a little while when Jamie sticks her head inside the curtain and tells them they need to say their goodbyes. The two of them offer a few more encouraging words and then leave.

After they're gone, I realize the powerful connection I have with my teammates, especially McGee, Pagano, and Kermit. We became friends as freshmen and now

CHAPTER 2

we're seniors. With the ER relatively quiet, I reflect on all the good times I've had playing tennis at both Mount Olive Junior College and UNC–Wilmington. I owe a lot to the sport. Playing tennis has financially helped put me through college and motivated me to do well and stay in school.

Realizing that I may never play tennis again, I start to reflect on how I came to love the sport. The summer I turned ten, I collected empty soda bottles from the waterfront, ditches, and trash cans around Washington Park. Glass bottles garnered five cents apiece when deposited at Clover Farm Country Store, and after weeks of collecting them, I happily walked into Malison's Sporting Goods Store and purchased a wooden Cambridge racket for seven dollars. My parents wouldn't let me ride my bicycle across town to the public tennis courts, so, for the longest time, my makeshift tennis court and hitting partner was the brick wall of the municipal building next door to our house. But in my imagination, I faced off against greats such as "Rocket" Rod Laver and Ilie "Nasty" Nastase.

As luck would have it, two years later in 1974, I watched in jubilation as a demolition crew destroyed a three-story apartment building that sat a block away from our house. In its place, the town constructed two tennis courts, shuffleboard courts, and a playground.

A group of older men monopolized the courts on the weekends, so for me, it was frustrating to have new tennis courts right across the street from our house and not be able to use them very often. As a result, my first experience playing on the new courts involved picking up tennis balls that the old farts had left or hit over the fence. Then I would get up early before school or go out late at night and serve buckets and buckets of these balls. This humbling practice paid dividends as a player throughout my career.

Pulling me back to the present, Jamie and Phyllis appear through the curtain and flip me onto my back.

"Thank you, Jesus," I whisper to myself, relieved to be looking up. They unbuckle the large straps that hold the Stryker frame together. "What's going on?" I ask.

"Dr. Anthony is here to fit you with a brace," Jamie replies.

As the two nurses finish removing the straps, in walk both Dr. Sheldon and Dr. Anthony. Dr. Anthony introduces himself to Mama and Daddy and then to me. "Michael, I'm Dr. Anthony, a neurosurgeon who works in the hospital. I'm here to fit you with a brace to help stabilize your neck."

As Phyllis escorts my parents out of the room, Jamie stands at the head of the bed and Dr. Sheldon at the foot of it. Together, they lift the top frame of the bed off me. Once it's removed, Dr. Sheldon gently places his hands on the sides of my head and tells me to keep my head still. Jamie rolls a large overhead light next to my bed. Through the reflection in the lens, I see a distorted image of my face and chest. The hospital gown I'm wearing is a far cry from the outfit I had on just hours ago.

Dr. Anthony rolls next to me on a stool and pulls a stainless steel cart with him. Out of the corner of my eye, I see metal instruments partially covered with a

CHAPTER 2

green towel. Jamie sits across from Dr. Anthony. While Dr. Sheldon holds my head still, Jamie takes an electric trimmer and cuts the hair away from my temples and slightly above and behind both ears. Finally, she uses a razor to shave the stubble that the trimmer left behind.

"I'm confused," I tell Dr. Anthony. "I thought I was getting fitted with a brace to keep my neck from moving."

"You are," he replies. "I'm fitting you with a Trippi-Wells brace or halo that attaches to your head and helps stabilize your neck."

As Jamie finishes shaving the four spots on my head, Dr. Anthony grabs a large syringe from the table. He sticks the needle into my right temple then my left. I feel the medicine penetrate and burn my skin. He moves the needle to the back of my head and numbs those two sites. Next, I feel Dr. Anthony apply something cold to the shaven areas of my head. In the reflection of the overhead light, I see him swab those spots with iodine, which is an antiseptic, then toss the gauze pad onto the tray. I finally put the pieces together and realize what's getting ready to happen. Dr. Anthony takes the halo off the cart and carefully guides it into place. Dr. Sheldon removes his hands from the sides of my head and holds the brace in place.

The brace, a U-shaped titanium bar about an inch thick, fits over the top of my head. Four threaded stainless steel pins, each three inches long, attach to the bar. The threaded pins line up directly with the four shaven spots on my head. While Dr. Sheldon holds the apparatus in place, Dr. Anthony uses his fingers to begin tightening the screws. He tells me that it won't hurt, but I'll feel some pressure against my skull. As the screws break the skin, I can hear the razor-sharp threads cutting through my flesh. Dr. Anthony grabs two wrenches off the cart and continues to twist the pins into my skull while Dr. Sheldon holds my head in place. The sound of these pencil-sized screws penetrating my skull is traumatizing.

Dr. Anthony finishes securing the brace by fitting me with a hard-shell vest and inserting four metal rods that connect the vest to my halo. Once he's done, I feel violated. I'm defenseless against anyone or anything. My cocky self-image has been stripped away. I can't even lift my hand to wipe the tears from my eyes. As the tears creep into my mouth, down my neck, then abruptly disappear, it's a harsh reminder that I have no sensation from the neck down.

CHAPTER 3

AFTER THE PROCEDURE, I'm moved off the Stryker frame and onto a gurney where I'm transported to the Critical Care Unit (CCU). It's close to nine o'clock when I reach my room. Once there, I'm reunited with my parents, and I see my brother and Sharon for the first time. Lee has made the trip by himself from Washington to Wilmington. Sharon is standing beside him, visibly upset. No doubt Mama and Daddy have told her about my paralysis. She grabs my limp hand and lifts it to her face. Distressed she says, "I came to the emergency room as soon as I got the news."

"Who told you?" I ask.

"Your roommate David called my apartment and told my roommate you were in a car accident," she replies.

Sharon tells me that while she was waiting in the ER, an unfamiliar woman asked if she could pray for her. After doing so, the woman anointed Sharon's head with oil. I wonder if this was the same women who thought I was her son? I try looking into Sharon's eyes, but she's looking at the large metal contraption screwed

47

into my skull. "Are you in a lot of pain?" she asks.

"No," I respond.

Once I'm off the gurney and in a hospital bed, Dr. Anthony attaches the halo to bed-based traction. He hooks one end of a steel cable into the top of the U-shaped brace and the other end runs through a pulley and hangs to the floor with twenty-five pounds of weight attached to it. When he finishes, Dr. Anthony says he'll see me tomorrow during his rounds. The sheer amount of weight used to stabilize my neck instantly produces a deep throbbing pain. But it's hard to distinguish whether the agonizing pain is from my broken neck or from the traction—or both.

To accommodate my parents, the hospital staff brings in two sleeper recliners. My roommates, McGee, Pagano, and Piepmeyer, unselfishly offer to let my parents stay at our apartment. My parents graciously decline the offer but ask if they can stop by and shower in the evenings.

Not long after I'm placed in traction, a nurse walks in and introduces herself. "Hey there! My name is Tricia. I'll be your nurse tonight." She rolls a table next to my bed, and out of the corner of my eye, I see her place two syringes on the table.

"What are those for?" I ask.

"For pain," she replies.

Tricia pulls the large curtain that hangs from the ceiling and walks it around the bed, giving me some privacy. Then she draws back the bedsheet and gently rolls up my gown, exposing my legs. She swabs a small area of my left thigh with an alcohol wipe, grabs a syringe off the table, and removes the cap. I lose sight

CHAPTER 3

of the syringe, but I wait, expecting the painful stick. It doesn't come, which is a poignant reminder that I have no feeling in my legs. She places the empty syringe on the table and plunges the second one into my leg.

"What's in the shots?" I ask.

"Demerol," she answers.

Tricia pulls the curtain open slightly and says, "I'll be right back." Moments later, she returns holding a small plastic bag. She opens it and pulls out a pair of long white stockings. When I ask her why I have to wear stockings, she explains that they're to prevent blood clots from forming in my legs. She rolls the compression stockings up my legs then pulls the curtain fully open.

As a warm feeling moves up my neck and into my face, I notice that the pain in my head and neck is starting to diminish. Feeling tongue-tied, I turn to my mom and say, "I think those shots are making me sleepy."

As I watch Tricia change an IV bag, it's like she's moving in slow motion. With her every movement, streaks of white light follow behind her.

Mama leans over the bed railing, smiles, and says something to me. But I can't hear her, and her face looks distorted. It's the last thing I remember for two days.

○ ○ ○

On Thursday, November 21, the sound of alarms beeping loudly nearby startles me awake. Disoriented at first, I quickly realize where I am and why I'm here. Tricia scampers into the room and greets me with a touch of sarcasm, "Well, hello, sleepyhead. It's about time you woke up."

"What's beeping?" I ask in a gravelly voice. My throat is as dry as a desert.

"That's the heart monitor behind you," she responds.

I clear my throat, "Is there something wrong with my heart?"

"No, it's beeping because your resting heart rate sometimes drops below the default setting on the machine," she answers. "I've never had a patient with a resting heart rate in the thirties."

"Why is it so low?" I ask out of curiosity.

"It's probably a combination of being in good shape and suffering from bradycardia, a symptom of neurogenic shock."

Tricia resets the monitor and leaves the room. Shortly afterward, Sharon and my parents walk in. They're happy to see me awake. I smile and make eye contact with Sharon. When she smiles back, I see her dimples.

"How long have you been awake?" Mama asks.

"Just a few minutes," I tell her. "How long have I been asleep?"

"Off and on for two days, son," Daddy answers.

"You're kidding me!" I respond.

"No, we're not. You've cried out in pain several times, but I don't think you were actually awake," Mama adds.

"What time is it?" I ask.

"A little after seven o'clock in the evening," Daddy informs me.

Tricia walks back in the room and announces that it's time for my suppository, so my parents and Sharon step out while Tricia closes the curtain. As she pulls

CHAPTER 3

down the bedsheet and lifts my hospital gown, a jolt of electricity shoots from my torso through my legs, causing me to scream with pain.

"What did you do?" I yell.

"I'm sorry. I just pulled up your gown," she apologizes.

"It felt like you poked me with a cattle prod!"

"Your skin is hypersensitive right now, so sometimes the slightest brush of the skin can cause painful muscle spasms. I believe the condition is called allodynia," she explains.

"What else is going on with me?" I wonder out loud.

Tricia carefully begins taking off my diaper while answering the question. She tells me I have a Foley catheter in my bladder that attaches to a urine bag below my bed. I'm also wearing compression stockings and have weights attached to my halo. I say that I vaguely remember her putting stockings on my legs two days earlier.

Once the diaper is off, she takes a suppository and places it up my rectum, which causes another rigid spasm. Once the spasm subsides, she puts the diaper back on and lets me know the suppository will take effect shortly. When she leaves the room, Mama, Daddy, and Sharon return.

With concern, my dad says, "What's hurting, son? I heard you yell out a few minutes ago."

"When the nurse lifted my gown, it made my muscles spasm. It felt like I was being electrocuted."

"Are you in pain now?" he asks.

"No, the spasms didn't last long."

However, half an hour later, the muscles inside me spontaneously ignite. Every few seconds, the pain intensifies, getting hotter and hotter. I tell Daddy that I'm hurting.

"Where are you hurting, son? Is it your neck?"

"No, it's deep inside me. It's everywhere!" I shout in distress.

Within seconds, the pain is unbearable. It's like someone is plunging hot serrated knives straight from a forge deep inside my body. I feel like I'm burning to death from the inside out. When I shriek from the pain again, Daddy rushes out of the room to find a nurse. Sharon squeezes my hand while my mother presses the call button.

"This must be what's happening in his sleep," Mama says to Sharon.

Daddy races back into the room with Tricia right behind him. She pulls out two syringes from the pocket of her uniform and plunges them into my thigh. I wait in anguish for the Demerol to take effect. Once it does, the furnace inside me is extinguished and sleep prevails.

○ ○ ○

On Friday, November 22, three days after my accident, I'm elated when my legs twitch on their own. However, Dr. Anthony is quick to inform us that the leg movements are involuntary muscle spasms, which is a symptom of spinal shock. We learn that my body will experience spinal shock for the next six to eight weeks. Until this period is over, it's difficult to know what voluntary movements

CHAPTER 3

will return. I also find out that the deep, burning sensations occurring without warning are neuropathic, another complication of neurogenic shock.

A few days into my recovery, the combination of neuropathic pain and the constant flow of Demerol through my veins has me in a hazy fog. My brother, along with several friends come and go without me noticing. When I'm awake, the amount of Demerol in my system directly correlates to my ability to carry on a conversation. The drug produces periods of deep sleep but also terrifying nightmares.

One recurring nightmare involves a roller coaster. In my dream, four or five empty wooden roller-coaster cars continuously circle a huge loop. At the bottom of the loop, a section of track is missing, and in its place, my body is stretched across the gap. As the heavy cars thunder toward me, I try to break free, but I can't move. I shout, "Help! Somebody help me!" Just before the car's cast-iron wheels hit my body, I wake up screaming.

Even worse than that, my physical reaction to the dream triggers neuropathic pain. The nightmares get so intense that my father asks Dr. Anthony if he can increase my pain medication. He says no because I'm already taking the maximum dose he can prescribe.

By Monday, November 25, Daddy is so desperate to put an end to the nightmares and ease my pain that he hires a hypnotist. I'm introduced to a white-haired gentleman, but I don't remember his name or being hypnotized. After the hypnosis, the searing pain in my central nervous system remains, but the roller-coaster nightmare subsides. However, in its place, I experience other dreams. The viewfinder

THE VIEWFINDER

produces one vibrant image from my past that reveals a single moment that changed the direction of my life—at least until the car accident.

In the image, I'm standing face-to-face with my coworker Johnny, ready for a fight. Standing to my left is another coworker named Roy. A large, rotating metal table covered with carpet is in front of us. It's August 1980, and I had just graduated from high school two months earlier.

Daddy had helped me land a job at Edinburgh Sawmill on the outskirts of Washington. The Dunleavys who ran the mill were family friends that lived across the street from us. My job at the sawmill was simple: as wooden blocks fell from a conveyer belt onto the rotating table, I had to stack any blocks that were free of knots onto pallets and throw the others onto a conveyer belt that discarded them into a dumpster outside. Sorting and stacking blocks was monotonous and borderline tortuous to me, but Johnny could spot blocks free of knots and grab and stack them twice as fast as me or Roy.

Standing around the table, it was hard for me not to dwell on the fact that three months earlier, I was on my way to college with a tennis scholarship in my back pocket. The long hours of practice and my successful high school career had drawn the attention of the tennis coach at Mount Olive Junior College. Unfortunately, just days before signing my scholarship, I received a call from the coach that my high school grades were too weak to grant me admission. In other words, I was too stupid to get into college. So while many of my classmates headed off to college, I was making minimum wage doing a mindless task that required no formal education.

CHAPTER 3

Angered by the circumstance I found myself in, I looked over and saw Johnny enjoying himself as he threw the imperfect blocks of wood behind his back onto the conveyer belt like he was one of the Harlem Globetrotters. Being a competitive athlete, I began throwing blocks behind my back, starting a friendly game with Johnny. In fact, we were smiling at each other and having a few minutes of fun doing a job that was anything but enjoyable.

While we were kidding around, I noticed a piece of frayed carpet dangling from the table. Occasionally, the edges of the carpet that lined the table unraveled and needed trimming. Without thinking, I pulled out my box cutter and snipped off the piece of carpet. But unbeknownst to me, this was Johnny's job—and his alone—so when he saw me cut off the tattered piece of carpet, the smile immediately left his face. With two blocks in his hands, he approached me—his face just inches from mine—and stared at me with cold, blank eyes. I looked back at him confused and shrugged my shoulders as if to say, *What's up with you?* He said nothing, but the look he gave me sent chills down my spine. Face-to-face with Johnny, I realized right then and there that my life was going to take one of two paths. If I stayed at this job, or even in this town, I would be heading toward a lifetime of mediocrity.

At the end of my shift that day, I tracked down Tommy and told him about the incident with Johnny. He apologized and explained that Johnny was good at his job but had a history of run-ins with law enforcement. After learning that, I told Tommy I wouldn't be coming back to work.

Driving home that day, I asked myself two questions: First, how did I get to this point in my life? The answer to that question could be traced back to the eighth grade. When most of my friends started taking advanced math classes, I did not. When I got to high school, I decided to take Algebra I to join my smarter friends, but a month later, I was failing the class. Because I was so far behind, the teacher started sending me to the library so I wouldn't be a distraction to the rest of the class. These daily trips to the library were a stinging reminder that I wasn't very smart.

Renowned motivational speaker Zig Ziglar best described what I experienced in that class. Ziglar coined the acronym SNIOP: Susceptible to the Negative Influences of Other People. He believed SNIOP was a self-fulfilling prophecy, which meant that every time the teacher sent me to the library, it reaffirmed my belief that I was stupid. As my self-esteem plummeted, I lost confidence in my ability to do math, setting the self-fulfilling prophecy in motion: I believed I was a failure in math, so I was. And that failing algebra grade on my high school transcript was the reason I was throwing wood blocks alongside a convicted felon and not playing college tennis.

The second question I asked myself was: If I knew working at the sawmill was taking me down the wrong path in life, then what was the right path? And what obstacles were standing in the way of my hopes and dreams? The answer to that question was me. From an academic standpoint, I was standing in my own way because I was too afraid to try. I was afraid that I might try my best and still fail.

CHAPTER 3

So I reasoned that if I *didn't* try my best and failed a test or an assignment, I could just say I didn't really try; therefore, I didn't have to feel disappointed in myself. This rationalization that produced my poor work ethic in high school had become the life preserver I used to keep my fragile self-esteem afloat. Driving home after quitting my job at the sawmill, I realized that this life preserver was slowly taking me to the bottom of the ocean. I was drowning.

When I arrived home, I stepped out of my car with an obvious goal in mind: I would call the tennis coach at Mount Olive Junior College and plead with him to hold my scholarship so I could take the courses needed to meet the school's admissions requirements. I made a promise to myself that for every hour I played tennis during the day, I would spend two hours studying at night.

THE VIEWFINDER

CHAPTER 4

On Tuesday morning, one week after becoming a quadriplegic, I meet my physical therapist, Dannie. The first thing I recognize is her Boston accent. Daddy notices her quick wit when she strikes up a conversation with my parents. Recognizing a kindred spirit, he dives into his repertoire of jokes to break the ice, and it creates an immediate rapport between them.

Dannie lets us know that she'll be working with me twice a week to move my arms and legs through range-of-motion exercises, which will help keep my muscles pliable and slow down the atrophy process. During Dannie's initial evaluation, she has me try to move my fingers, toes, arms, and legs.

"I've tried repeatedly to move my arms and legs, and I can't do it!" I complain. "It's like my head is attached to someone else's body."

Dannie immediately validates my deflated outlook. "It's nawmal to feel this way, so don't beat yuhself up. I want ya to relax and watch me while I put yuh ahms and legs through their nawmal range of motion."

CHAPTER 4

After watching Dannie move my limbs back and forth, I quickly look away in disgust.

"Michael, keep wahtchin'!" she demands.

"Why? What's the point?" I gripe.

"Because seein' yuh ahms and legs move will aid in yuh recovery," she replies reassuringly.

I do as I'm told and observe my listless limbs moving to and fro. At the end of my physical therapy session, I'm disheartened and angry. Dannie tries, unsuccessfully, to leave me with some encouraging words. Then she reminds me that she'll see me on Thursday.

○ ○ ○

The following morning, I receive more depressing news. Over the past couple of days, the nurses have gently encouraged me to eat since I've scarcely done so in the last week. Frankly, the sight and smell of food are repulsive to me. But today I learn that Dr. Anthony has left word with the nursing staff that if I don't start eating, he's going to order a feeding tube. *That's all I need is another hose impaling my body,* I grumble silently to myself.

Hearing the disheartening news, I scream in anger, "I'm already mentally hanging on by a freakin' thread, and now they want to shove another tube inside me?"

Daddy talks me down and assures me that I'm not getting a feeding tube. To try to get me to eat, he brings me a McDonald's hamburger and french fries for lunch. I attempt to eat more than a few bites, but it's like chewing salty cardboard.

THE VIEWFINDER

Midday brings a barrage of nurses coming in to change IV bags, reset the heart monitor, and empty my urine bag. By late afternoon, I welcome the two shots of Demerol that put me out of my misery.

Shortly before seven o'clock, nurse Tricia wakes me up. "You have a visitor!" she says excitedly then abruptly leaves the room.

I find her behavior odd. *Why tell me I have a visitor and then rush out of the room?* I look over at my parents, who are also confused. My second thought is that whoever it is has timed the visit perfectly because my narcotic-driven stupor has worn off, but I'm not in a lot of pain.

I hear nurses chattering in the hallway and someone on a walkie-talkie. Tricia pokes her head in the doorway, flashes me a huge grin, then disappears. Curious, Daddy gets up and walks toward the door to check things out. But before he can get there, two large men enter my room. One of them resembles Arnold Schwarzenegger; the other one *is* Arnold Schwarzenegger! For a split second, I think I'm hallucinating, but I quickly realize that I'm not when both men walk over to my parents and introduce themselves—as if Arnold Schwarzenegger needs an introduction. He extends his sympathies to my parents.

Arnold walks over to my bed and introduces himself and his stunt double, Peter Kent. Arnold leans forward, placing one hand on the bed rail and the other one gently on my shoulder. Out of the corner of my eye, I see his clenched hand wrapped around the bed railing. It's the size of a small baseball glove! Below his hand is a stuffed animal: a lion. *How fitting,* I think. *Arnold is the king of the*

CHAPTER 4

jungle in the world of powerlifting and action movies, and beside him sits a stuffed lion someone has given me as a get-well gesture.

"Michael, how ahh you doing?" he asks in his thick Austrian accent.

"Okay," I reply.

"I heard about yahr ahccident, and I'm very sahry it hahppened."

"How did you know I was in an accident?" I ask.

"You hahve friends in high places," he says jokingly. "I heeuh you're uh tennis playah for ze university."

"*Was* a tennis player," I say despondently.

Before leaving, Arnold gives me an autographed picture of himself as the Terminator and tells me, "Michael, I hahve faced and ovehcome ahdversity in my life, and you will do ze same. You ahr uh fightah. Just take it one day at uh time and fight!"

I take these words to heart, and "just take it one day at a time and fight" becomes my father's rallying cry for me when things get tough. After the visit, I name my stuffed lion Arnold.

Schwarzenegger's visit sends a buzz around the hospital. Nurses hear rumors of a local TV crew showing up and wanting to know why Arnold Schwarzenegger is visiting the hospital. But for as much hoopla as Schwarzenegger's visit generates, nobody notices Dr. Bachner's visit the following night—no one except me.

Saul Bachner is a professor in the Education Department at UNC–Wilmington. Hailing from the Bronx, Dr. Bachner reminds me of actor Billy Crystal. He's one of the most beloved and well-respected professors on campus. I enjoy his class, Education 201, immensely. He's a walking sports encyclopedia and frequently integrates sports analogies and trivia into his lectures. Before my accident, I was hanging on for dear life to a B average in his class.

"Michael Jarvis, are you awake?" His distinct voice prompts me to open my eyes. He calls me by my first and middle names as if they are one name.

"Hey, Dr. Bachner!" I say with surprise.

"How are you feeling, champ? Are you in a lot of pain?"

"No, I'm good, Dr. Bachner."

"You tennis players have such good poker faces." He grins then adds sarcastically, "Look, I know you're worried sick because you're missing my class."

"Yeah, I don't think I'm going to make the final exam, Dr. Bachner," I say with a slight smile.

"Don't worry about the exam. You've earned the B in my class." After a momentary pause, he continues, "Michael Jarvis, I have a favorite quote I live by: 'Don't hurry. Don't worry. Take time to smell the roses.'" Then he leans over the bed, looks in my eyes, and says, "Don't worry. You're going to beat this." Then he winks at me, turns, and leaves.

Shortly after his departure, my parents return from having dinner in the hospital cafeteria. I tell them about my visit with Dr. Bachner and his uncharacteristic decision to give me a complete grade in his class. They're disappointed that they missed seeing him.

CHAPTER 4

When eight o'clock rolls around, the Demerol begins wearing off. Daddy sees the telltale signs of pain and starts searching the hallway for my nurse. Several minutes later, Tricia shows up with two shots of Demerol. As I wait for my fix to kick in, I think about how nice it was not only for Dr. Bachner to give me a B for the course but also to deliver the news in person. *Although he barely knows me, he had enough compassion to visit me,* I think to myself.

On the other hand, the guys I feel closest to—the ones I've spent countless hours with on and off the tennis court—I have yet to see by my bedside because I'm in a Demerol-driven sleep every time they stop by. All I know is that I miss them. As teammates, we share a highly competitive bond. We all want to be the best, which means we must defeat each other on our way to achieving that goal. We're all cocky on some level, and most, if not all of us, value our bodies; it's the vessel through which our talent manifests. As college athletes, the thought of being paralyzed is too scary to think about, so seeing me this way hits too close to home. Therefore, I understand why my teammates might be staying away. I would probably do the same thing. I tell myself the fewer people who come to visit, the better. That way I don't have to put up a tough-guy facade, which I just don't have in me.

With my teammates, we generally keep our relationships lighthearted, joking around and teasing each other. Obvious displays of love and compassion for one another are not cool. Sadly, this same lackluster approach is also how I treat my parents. For a long time, I have neglected to tell my parents that I love them, and living away at college for the past few years has made it easy to escape saying those

THE VIEWFINDER

three words. *Even now as I lie in this bed paralyzed with my parents by my side almost twenty-four hours a day, I cannot bring myself to say those words. But why?* I wonder.

My parents have sacrificed so much for me and my brother. For years, Daddy has juggled three jobs: He manages an ABC Store in Chocowinity. He's the town clerk of Washington Park. And on Sundays, he cleans and buffs the floors of the ABC Store in Washington. My mom has cooked and cleaned and worn the same few outfits for well over a decade just to save money so that Lee and I could earn a higher education. As I lie in the bed chastising myself, I look over and see Mama sitting across from me wearing one of my discarded, old V-neck sweater vests over the top of a dated blouse. I'm disgusted with myself, and my selfish narcissism sickens me. Why is it only now, in my greatest time of need, that I'm recognizing how much I've neglected my relationship with them? When I'm clearheaded, my guilt is palpable. Reluctantly, or perhaps with a sense of relief, I welcome the reprieve from my shame that the intravenous Demerol provides every few hours.

It's been nine days since my accident, and I realize that I'm becoming addicted to Demerol. Consciously, I want the drug flowing through my veins because I can't tolerate the intense neuropathic pain that envelops me. Subconsciously, I want the liquid poison because I can't deal with the reality that I'm faced with every day. At this point, I can't distinguish between the physical pain from my injury and the psychological pain that occurs when the Demerol leaves my bloodstream. Once I have this addictive opioid flowing through my veins, my pain diminishes and my worries vanish, only to return a few hours later. It's the vicious cycle of an addict.

CHAPTER 4

○ ○ ○

On the morning of December 3, I experience a tremendous breakthrough in my recovery. When Dannie shows up for my physical therapy session, Mama and Daddy step out to give us some privacy. As is customary, Dannie begins manipulating my limbs through their range of motion. After exercising my left leg, she puts it down and notices my toes move ever so slightly.

"Did ya just have a leg spasm?" she asks in her Boston accent.

"I don't think so."

Her eyes widen as she joyfully states, "Ya just moved the toes on yuh left foot!"

"Don't do this to me, Dannie. Don't give me false hope," I beg.

She carefully removes my compression stocking and lifts my left leg up high enough so I can see my toes. "I want ya to focus on tryin' to move yuh toes," she says.

I look at my toes, close my eyes, and visualize them moving.

"Theyah! Ya just moved 'em again!" she squeals.

I quickly open my eyes, but my toes are motionless. I gaze at Dannie in desperation. She encourages me to try again, this time with my eyes open. Following her instructions, I stare intently at my foot, willing my toes to move, and then it happens. My big toe and the two toes beside it move ever so slightly. I can't feel them moving, but I see it with my own eyes. It's such a weird feeling!

She grabs my hand and pats it, "I'm so proud of ya!"

But in my mind, there's nothing for me to be proud of; I don't even know how I did it. Even so, I do know that what I just experienced is a blessing. I ask

THE VIEWFINDER

Dannie to wait around a few minutes for my parents to return so we can share this accomplishment with them together. She hangs around for several minutes but reluctantly has to leave and take care of other patients. But she leaves my compression stocking off so I can share this triumph with my parents. Half an hour later when Mama and Daddy return, I call them over to my bed.

"Daddy, hold up my left leg and watch my toes," I say.

Taken aback by my enthusiasm, Daddy eagerly grabs my leg and lifts it up while I move those same three toes. Afterward, Daddy puts my leg down, runs his fingers through my hair, and, with tears in his eyes, just smiles at me. At that moment, I feel like the small boy in the mirror whose loving father is taming his hair before church. This loving gesture is the first display of affection my father has shown me in many years.

For my father, seeing my toes move is a bittersweet moment. Up to this point, I was unaware that for the past few days, Daddy has been trying to convince Dr. Anthony that I'm not physically ready to leave the hospital and transfer to a rehabilitation facility. I soon learn that Dr. Anthony believes I'm stable and ready for the services only a comprehensive rehab center can provide. That I can now move my toes only reinforces Dr. Anthony's position.

Sure enough, Daddy loses the argument with Dr. Anthony, and it's decided that I'll be transferred to Pitt County Regional Rehabilitation Center in Greenville, North Carolina. As a last-ditch effort to protect my precarious health, Daddy requests that the hospital airlift me to the rehab center, but his request falls on deaf ears.

CHAPTER 4

On December 5, sixteen days after my accident, my family says goodbye to the dedicated staff members who have taken excellent care of me. Dr. Anthony comes by my room early in the morning to disconnect the cable that attaches my halo to the weights below my bed. While he tightens my pins with a wrench, I ask him how long I'll have to wear the halo and vest. He tells me around four to six weeks, so, essentially, until my neck heals.

Daddy still has reservations about my departure from the hospital, but we're excited to be moving on to the next chapter in my recovery. An ambulance is waiting for us outside the emergency room doors. Before leaving my room, the nurse gives me two shots of Demerol for the two-and-a-half-hour road trip. As I exit the hospital, the chilly December air takes my breath away. My next few breaths hurt my lungs, but it feels so refreshing just to be outside again.

For the trip to Greenville, my mother accompanies me in the ambulance along with Arnold, my stuffed lion. Daddy tells me it's a good thing Mama can ride in the ambulance because there's no room for her in the car. My roommates McGee and Pagano have helped him load up the family car with my belongings from the apartment. Daddy will follow behind the ambulance, and when we all arrive at the rehab center, he and Mama will get me admitted then the two of them will head home to Washington Park.

The EMTs transporting me say that if my pain increases, I should let them know, and they'll turn on the siren and lights and pick up speed. As they load me into the ambulance, I'm thankful to be leaving New Hanover Regional Medical

Center and putting the memory of being rushed into its emergency room far behind me.

As we make our way onto US Highway 17, I recall a discussion I had with Dannie about what I can expect to happen during my rehabilitative stay. She said that rehab is like going to school to learn how to reuse your body. The facility has specialized therapies to teach patients how to live with quadriplegia. To me, being labeled a quadriplegic sounds unalterable and irreversible, so I put that word out of my mind and instead focus on the rehabilitation process ahead of me.

As early as I can remember, I have enjoyed visualizing how things will unfold before I experience them. When I played Little League, I would get dressed in the morning for a late afternoon game, which drove my mom crazy. I would warm up in the backyard, throwing and fielding balls to myself, taking batting practice, and running makeshift bases. Eventually I would get tired, so I'd lay in the grass and visualize hitting the ball out of the park and making the game-winning tag at the plate.

Now it's time for me to visualize rebuilding my body. Looking around inside the ambulance, I see Mama sitting next to the paramedic, reading a Danielle Steel book. The paramedic, who looks to be in his late twenties, is carefully studying my medical chart. By now the Demerol is at full strength. I close my eyes and try to get some sleep, hoping it will make the time pass quickly.

Twenty minutes into the ride, I'm wide awake and having some discomfort: my right arm is spasming. The stretcher I'm lying on has limited cushion, so I can

CHAPTER 4

only assume it's the reason my vest is cutting into my shoulder. I tell the paramedic what's going on, so he pulls back the blanket I'm cocooned in and checks my vest. He notices a red spot forming where the vest is rubbing against my shoulder blade. He turns me slightly on my left side and places two pillows underneath me. That eases the spasms a bit, and provides some added padding.

To take my mind off the painful spasms, I focus on something Dr. Anthony reiterated to me and my parents before we left. He said my injury is classified as "incomplete," meaning that my spinal cord is not totally severed, so there's a possibility that I could regain even more motor function. With this thought in mind, I promise myself that from my first day at the rehab center to my last, I will have the mindset of Henry Ford, who is credited with saying, "Whether you think you can or you can't, either way, you're right." I decide then and there that I won't waste precious time or energy on negative thoughts and things I can't control.

Time passes slowly on the ride to Greenville. At one point, I look over and make eye contact with Mama. She raises her eyebrows at me and asks, "Are you hurting?"

"Not too much," I respond.

When she smiles, the words *I love you, Mama* are on the tip of my tongue, but they don't leave my lips. She buries her head back into her book, and I realize that I've missed my opportunity.

Every half hour, the paramedic checks my vitals. When he removes the blood pressure cuff from my arm, he says, for a third time, "Let me know if we need to turn on the siren and pick up the pace."

"You guys like to go fast, don't you?" I reply.

"Only when it's life or death," he says, grinning.

"This vest is still digging into my shoulder."

The paramedic squeezes the radio receiver attached to his chest. "Jeremy, we need to rock and roll," he tells the ambulance driver. Immediately, the motor revs, the siren sounds, and the lights reflect off the ambulance's back windows.

Mama looks at me with a shocked look that says, "I hope your daddy can keep up!"

I return her look with a smile. While we speed toward Greenville, I try to think positive thoughts: *Moving to the rehab center means I'll be closer to my brother and grandmother, who both live in Washington. Lee has only been able to visit me in the hospital a couple of times because of his engineering job, and Gramma was unable to visit me because she no longer drives. Also, for the first time in three weeks, my parents will sleep in their own bed. And finally, Christmas is coming and the fall semester at UNC–Wilmington is wrapping up, which means Sharon and I will have more time to spend together.* These thoughts make me excited to start my journey of rebuilding my body.

CHAPTER 5

It's midafternoon when we pull underneath the entrance to Pitt County Regional Rehabilitation Center. The sun is beaming through the skylight of the ambulance, and I'm already looking forward to a second glimpse of the blue sky when I exit the vehicle. From the chill in the air, I can tell winter is settling in around eastern North Carolina. I can also tell the Demerol I took when I left Wilmington is wearing off. In another hour, I'll be eagerly awaiting my fix, but for now, my excitement of being at the rehab center pushes aside the encroaching pain.

While the paramedics prepare to remove me from the ambulance, an administrator walks out of the rehab center and greets my mom. After parking the car, my dad joins them under the entryway.

"Hi, I'm Bo Bowen," he says to the administrator and extends his hand.

"Fran Meadows," she replies with a smile while taking his outstretched hand.

Turning to me, my dad asks, "How was the ride?"

"Not bad until the last few miles," I reply.

"So that was the reason for the siren and lights," he says.

"Yep," I concur.

Right away, my mom interjects, "He's complaining of painful spasms from the vest pushing against his shoulder blade."

"We'll get him some Demerol once he gets settled into his room," Daddy assures.

Once I'm out of the ambulance, Fran introduces herself to me. Looking me directly in the eye, she says some kind words designed to make me feel more at ease. As the paramedics roll me into the lobby, Fran escorts my parents to the admissions office. One paramedic pushes me to the back of the lobby, while the other one heads to the restroom. Lying on the gurney, I notice a portion of the lobby wall is glass, which provides a view of an outdoor common area. I watch as a few staff members and patients eat a late lunch outside.

The lobby itself is large but has a quaint feel to it with fifteen to twenty mahogany chairs and half a dozen love seats covered in patterns of burgundy, tan, and green. The chairs complement the plush Oriental rugs underneath them. The abstract artwork on the walls has a calming effect and is soothing to the eyes. It's easy to see that the person responsible for the room's design carefully crafted a space that would be both welcoming and comfortable. What *isn't* welcoming or comfortable is people passing by me while I lie on this gurney. I feel like Frankenstein with these bolts sticking out of my skull.

It takes a while, but my parents finally return to the lobby, then Fran leads our entourage down a wide hallway. We pass an elderly man who is slouched over

CHAPTER 5

in his wheelchair with his head leaning against the large wooden handrails that line both sides of the hallway. In a different context, he might appear drunk, but the wide padded seat belt that keeps him from sliding out of his chair leads me to believe he's had a stroke. A deep sense of compassion surges in me for this man. He could just as well be my father and not some stranger. Tears well up in my eyes, and I have to bite down on my bottom lip to keep it from trembling. This unexpected wave of emotion lingers as we travel down the hall. *Why am I so emotional? It's just an old man in a wheelchair,* I tell myself. *I don't even know his name!*

We turn and continue down another hallway. Off in the distance, through the low hum of nurses' chatter, I hear a deranged woman shrieking. Although I cannot decode her nonsensical noises, I can tell she's in distress. In my mind, I picture a woman with a disfigured face foaming at the mouth and clawing at the eyes of those who are detaining her. But soon, just off to my right, I see the hysterical figure near the entrance to her room. She isn't at all what I pictured. She's young—maybe twenty years old—and her hazel eyes are bursting with specks of gold. Her jet-black hair hangs just above her brow. Except for the dark semicircles under her eyes, she's almost pretty. As I pass in front of her, we make eye contact and she stops crying for a moment. Then she jerks her arms up and down, and I notice restraints tethering her wrists to the wheelchair. She tugs at them, looking desperately to me for help. I want to help her, but I can't even help myself!

As the distance between us grows, her cries of desperation fade, and I slowly begin to realize that my vision of rehab—people working out and trying to make

THE VIEWFINDER

the best of their prognosis—is nothing more than wishful thinking. The reality is that hospitals have sad, sick, and sometimes demented people in them. I wonder if my roommate will be a clone of either of the two individuals I just laid eyes on.

When we reach my room, the EMTs transfer me from the gurney to my new bed, which causes a rigid spasm throughout my body. It's clear—at least to me—that I need my fix, and I need it now! The two EMTs say goodbye and wish me luck. Mama unpacks the few things she brought with her in the ambulance, while Daddy leaves the room to find someone who can give me some pain medicine.

To focus on something other than my pain, I watch intently as my mom places get well cards on the table beside my bed. She places Arnold in my bed against the railing then reaches back into the bag and grabs a small stack of neatly folded clothes. Among them are the spandex tights I wore in the movie, providing me with a sober reminder of the life I used to have.

My room is semiprivate, which means a large retractable curtain separates my side from my roommate. Mama has already found out that his name is Rabbit, and I hope, for his sake, it's a nickname. Under normal circumstances, I would chuckle at the name, but until I get some Demerol, nothing is funny.

Daddy walks into the room with three people in tow. The older and taller of the two men steps forward and introduces himself. "Hello, Mr. Bowen, welcome to Pitt County Regional Rehabilitation Center," he says with a German accent. "I'm Dr. Alsentzer, the director of the facility. Patients call me Dr. A." Then he gestures with his hand and introduces his two physician's assistants, Mr. Bousman

CHAPTER 5

and Mr. Gregg. He tells me the three of them, along with a team of therapists, will monitor and evaluate my progress while I'm here.

Dr. A gives me a rundown of what my daily routine will look like at the rehab center. In the morning hours, I'll have physical therapy (PT) and occupational therapy (OT). After lunch, I'll attend group therapy followed by recreational therapy. If needed, I'll work with a psychologist for pain management and depression. Visiting hours are between five and nine o'clock in the evening. The whole time Dr. A is talking, all I can think about is getting those two shots of Demerol. When there's a momentary pause in his monologue, I ask, "Can I get some Demerol for the pain in my neck and shoulder?"

Taken aback by the bluntness of my request, he responds, "We do not prescribe Demerol at this facility."

"What does that mean?" I question.

"The strongest drug we prescribe for pain here is Tylenol," he states matter-of-factly.

"Tylenol!" I shout incredulously. "I've been receiving two shots of Demerol every four hours for the last three weeks!"

Despite my consternation, Dr. A calmly reiterates that Tylenol 3 is the strongest medication prescribed at the rehab center.

I can't believe what I'm hearing. Tylenol? That's it? I don't just have a headache; I have a fractured neck! What the hell kind of place is this?

By now, it's been four hours since my last dose of Demerol. Dr. Alsentzer steps

THE VIEWFINDER

into the hallway and flags down a nurse. Mama and Daddy follow him. Before Dr. A utters a word to my parents, he stops a nurse and says, "Will you get me 600 milligrams of Tylenol 3 and point two milligrams of clonidine?" Then he faces my parents and explains, "Your son does not need more Demerol. The Tylenol and clonidine I'm prescribing will ease most of his symptoms."

"So the Tylenol is prescription-strength?" Daddy asks.

"Yes, it is," Dr. Alsentzer replies. "It has codeine in it."

"What was the other drug you mentioned?" Mama inquires.

"Clonidine," Dr. A answers. "It will help with the withdrawal symptoms from the Demerol."

While Dr. Alsentzer and my parents converse in the hall, nobody seems to give a *damn* about the neuropathic pain frying my nerves and the tidal wave of nausea barreling up my GI tract and preparing to spew from my mouth. All I can think is: *God, where are you? How does a compassionate God allow someone to hurt this much?*

Mama and Daddy come back into the room. By now they're familiar with the meltdown that ensues when my Demerol wears off, so they commence the intervention. Mama tells me that Tylenol 3 is a prescription-strength pain medication, which is stronger than the over-the-counter drug. She also explains that Dr. Alsentzer is giving me another med for the nausea. She doesn't mention that it's a detox drug.

My brother, Lee, shows up around four thirty. By this time, the Tylenol 3 has knocked the edge off my pain, but I still feel lousy. Even so, seeing him puts a smile on my face. He quickly recognizes that I'm not in a good mood, so Daddy

CHAPTER 5

quietly informs him of the rehab center's policy of prescribing nothing stronger than Tylenol with codeine for pain.

I'm stunned when Lee defends the rehab's position, saying, "I get it. They don't want to produce a bunch of junkies who already have enough problems as it is."

"Are you saying I'm a junkie?" I counter defensively.

Emphatically, Lee says, "Of course not!" Although I disagree with my brother's stance, who am I to argue? I'm just the one experiencing the symptoms of opiate withdrawal: sweating, trembling, and hurting all over.

For the next couple of hours, we try, as a family, to enjoy each other's company. I listen as my brother talks about his challenges at work. Daddy jokingly tells us his three-week vacation is over, so he'll be returning to work tomorrow. I know I should feel grateful that my family is returning to some form of normalcy, but I'm not. I'm envious that they can go home, but I'm stuck here.

I hear a knock at the door, and a woman announces that she's from food services. Apparently, it's time for dinner. She retreats to the hallway and reappears with a food tray, placing it on the rolling table at the foot of my bed. As she has done for the past three weeks, my mother steps to the side of my bed to feed me. With the bravest face I can muster, I tell my family to go home—that I can get a nurse to feed me. While a part of them is reluctant to leave me, it has been a long day, and I know my parents are looking forward to having a home-cooked meal and spending the night in their own bed.

Before they leave, Mama finds a nurse who can help me with dinner. My brother says goodbye while my father combs his fingers through my hair and assures me that I'll be fine. For the first time since my accident, I will spend the night without one of my parents in the room with me. Although I hate to admit it, I have become emotionally dependent on them. And not just on my parents but the nurses too. My current condition is a constant reminder that my existence—and even my very survival—depends on the help of others. I gradually push this depressing thought aside and remind myself that my parents are only a short distance away if I need them.

When the nurse arrives to help me eat dinner, she removes the lid from the food tray, revealing baked chicken, mashed potatoes, and peas. It looks edible, but I'm just not hungry. I eat a few bites out of guilt since I know the nurse has taken time out of her busy schedule to help me. To remove some of the awkwardness I feel, I try to make small talk with her, starting with her name, which is Tammy. Her eyes light up as she talks about her twin boys. When she asks how I got injured, I don't go into details; I just say that I was in an automobile accident. After a few minutes, I politely ask her to take away my food tray. She obliges, but before she leaves, she asks if I need anything else. I say no, just some rest.

The Tylenol has given me enough relief that I feel like I can sleep. The room is quiet, and I have yet to lay eyes on my roommate. As I drift off to sleep, I recall the events of the day. I have traded in the traction bed at New Hanover Regional Medical Center for the regular hospital bed here at Pitt County Regional Rehabilitation Center. The ambulance ride from Wilmington to Greenville was

CHAPTER 5

mostly uneventful, with the highlight being a few precious breaths of fresh air entering and exiting the vehicle. I realize I've taken too many things in my young life for granted, my parents being at the top of the list. Before I drift off to sleep, I remember the drooling elderly man who was stooped over in his wheelchair and the demented girl pulling at her restraints. It makes me wonder, *What does fate have in store for me at this place?*

Later in the evening, the sound of people laughing wakes me up. When I open my eyes, I see a teenage girl and boy holding hands as they walk by the foot of my bed. The girl looks over at me and smiles apologetically, as if to say, "Sorry for intruding on your half of the room." When I look to my right, I notice several pairs of shoes underneath the curtain. The couple who passed by my bed pulls the curtain back just enough to make their presence known to Rabbit and his visitors.

I'm slightly disoriented and burning up. My first thought is that the flushness I feel is a side effect of the drug Dr. A prescribed for nausea, but there's also a heaviness in my chest that I can't explain. I try to take a deep breath but can't because of stabbing muscle spasms under my rib cage. I blame this discomfort on my vest, but with every passing minute, I feel worse. It doesn't take long for me to realize that the shortness of breath is not the vest—something is definitely wrong. Sweat is cascading down my face, and I feel like I'm breathing through a straw. I need help.

I can see the call button hanging around the bed railing only inches away from my useless right hand. Arnold, who's perched next to the button, is a reminder to me not to panic and to stay strong. I try calling out to the young couple standing just outside the curtain, but their backs are to me and my call for help is too faint for them to hear. I'm suffocating ten feet away from these people, and there's nothing I can do!

When there's a lull in the group's conversation, I say, "Help me!" as loud as my lungs allow, which is barely a whisper. The girl hears me, turns around, and immediately taps her boyfriend on the shoulder. When he looks at me, his eyes go wide, then he dashes out of the room. The girl rushes to my bedside as I gasp, "I can't breathe."

Before she can say a word, two nurses barge into the room. One grabs the stethoscope from around her neck and struggles to maneuver it under the close quarters of my vest.

"Michael, take a few deep breaths for me," she instructs. She closes her eyes as she moves the instrument from place to place across my chest. I catch a glimpse of her name tag; her name is Debra.

While Debra listens to my lungs, another nurse frantically grabs an oxygen mask off the back wall and places it over my nose and mouth. She bluntly asks Rabbit's guests to leave the room, and they comply. Then she attaches a blood pressure cuff to my arm and, with her stethoscope on the bend in my elbow, listens intently. "BP is seventy over fifty-two," she announces.

Debra shakes her head and immediately pushes my call button. "Call the trauma center, *stat*! Tell them we have a twenty-three-year-old male with a cervical spine

CHAPTER 5

injury in respiratory distress who possibly needs emergency intubation." Her tone is sharp, making it difficult to hide her concern, but the conviction in her voice tells me this is not her first rodeo. "Take slow, deep breaths for me," Debra says.

Although it feels like a twenty-pound dumbbell is sitting on my chest, the oxygen provides a small amount of relief, so I no longer feel like I'm suffocating.

The nurses' station buzzes my room, and a woman's voice announces, "We've contacted the ER, and a trauma team is on the way."

A trauma team? I think. *Why do I need a trauma team?*

Debra sits on the side of my bed and stares at me, anxiously waiting for the trauma team to show up. "By the way, I'm Debra. I bet this isn't how you wanted to spend your first night in rehab, is it?" she says as she tries to make light of the situation.

I have no way of answering her question: I can't speak. I can't even nod my head or gesture with my hands. All I can do is lie here and look at her.

After what seems like an eternity but was probably only a few minutes or so, I hear the sound of a fast-moving cart rolling down the hall before a doctor and nurse urgently enter my room. Both of them are panting.

Debra briefs the doctor on what's taken place in the past fifteen minutes. He asks her to locate my medical chart, so she leaves the room in search of my transfer paperwork. As the trauma nurse rolls a cart next to my bed, all I can think is that this feels like déjà vu. I'm facing the same chaotic scene I experienced in the emergency room back in Wilmington: the sights and sounds of doctors and nurses trying to save my life.

"Hey, Mr. Bowen. My name is Dr. Moore. I'm an ER doctor here at Pitt County Memorial Hospital," he says, still catching his breath. As Debra did, he places his stethoscope under the front of my vest and listens to me breathe. After several breaths, he and the trauma nurse turn me on my side. He places the scope to my back and has me take several more breaths. Then he pulls the scope away, and they gently roll me back over. Debra returns to the room and hands Dr. Moore my transfer papers, which he quickly skims through.

"Mr. Bowen, you have a buildup of fluid around your lungs," Dr. Moore informs me. "That's why it's so difficult for you to breathe." He reminds me of a teacher showing his students the relationship between cause and effect. He pauses and stares at me as if sizing up my level of distress. "Are you having any sharp pain when you breathe?" he asks.

"Yes, on my right side."

Turning to the trauma nurse, Dr. Moore says, "Jenna, let's set up for a nasal intubation. Get me a seven-millimeter nasotracheal tube, lidocaine spray and jelly, and two six-inch sterile Q-tips, please."

She immediately turns to the medical cart and starts opening and closing drawers and pulling out the requested items.

"Mr. Bowen, I need to put a tube up your nose and down into your lungs to make it easier for you to breathe," the doctor says while putting on a pair of sterile gloves.

He tells me to close my eyes and open my mouth. I feel the lidocaine spray land deep in my throat. Next, he applies a liberal coating of lidocaine jelly to a

CHAPTER 5

Q-tip and inserts it deep inside my nostril. While the lidocaine takes effect, the trauma nurse opens a sterile bag and pulls out a clear tube. She holds it up while Dr. Moore applies a generous amount of lidocaine jelly to it.

The tube must be twelve inches long. I close my eyes and prepare myself for the pain I'm about to experience. I silently pray to God, *Please have mercy on me!*

"Michael," Dr. Moore says, "you're going to feel an urge to gag and cough as the tube passes through your windpipe. This is normal. Just continue to swallow."

I feel the tube move smoothly through my nose, but as it inches toward my windpipe, my gag reflex kicks in. The pain is intense as I gag and fight for air.

"Don't fight the tube. Just swallow," Dr. Moore reiterates in a commanding voice.

I cough a few times, and the tube passes into my windpipe.

"You did great, Michael," Dr. Moore says reassuringly while Jenna nods her head in agreement.

Dr. Moore attaches the intubation tube to a respirator bag. As he squeezes the bag, my lungs begin filling with air, and I feel instant relief. Jenna reaches into the cart and pulls out a syringe and a vial of medicine. She fills the syringe and plunges it into my arm. Afterward, Dr. Moore directs her to take over for him. As Jenna pumps air into my lungs, Dr. Moore picks up the telephone in my room. I hear the words *CAT scan* leave his mouth.

The next thing I remember is waking up in an unfamiliar room. I am semiconscious, and Jenna is standing next to me. I don't see the respirator bag, but I know I'm not fully breathing on my own. At the foot of a gurney, I see Mama and Daddy. They're talking to Dr. Moore. I try to make out what's being said until I hear Dr. Moore say, "His condition is critical." When I hear those words, the small amount of fighting spirit I have left inside me disappears. *Why would God provide such hope just hours ago and now take it away?* I wonder. *I've lost all hope and my will to live.*

While my parents continue to talk with Dr. Moore, I close my eyes and digest the gravity of my condition. Facing the possibility of death truly tests one's faith. I ask myself: *Do I want to live like this, knowing that my chances of walking again are slim to none? I have no sensation from the neck down and no ability to go to the bathroom or feed myself. If the past three weeks of my existence are the prelude to the rest of my life, then I choose to die because this isn't living!* Convinced that I'll die if I give up and stop fighting, I choose my fate. There is no fight left in me.

Having made my choice, I decide that when I get a free moment alone with my parents, I will tell them how much I love them, thank them for all the sacrifices they've made for me, and tell them goodbye. When my parents and Dr. Moore walk over to the gurney, I try to ask him for a moment alone with my parents, but I have no ability to speak. Dr. Moore tells me he needs to insert a tube into my chest to drain fluid from around my right lung. There's no opportunity to say goodbye to my parents. Instead, it's a quick kiss on the forehead from Mama and a few swipes of my hair from Daddy, then they leave the room.

My next memory is waking up for a moment and seeing an unfamiliar doctor take away my vest. I wake up a second time with painful muscle spasms in

CHAPTER 5

my chest and abdomen then the gradual relief of the heavy pressure in my chest. Sometime later, I hear a drainage system suctioning my chest cavity and Dr. Moore say, "Okay, let's extubate."

It's almost midnight when I awake to two doctors standing next to my bed arguing with a third gentleman. I can't totally discern their conversation, but it has something to do with how best to set up the bed to accommodate the pins screwed into my head and the tube sticking out of my chest. I am fully awake yet totally confused and impatient. *Why all the fuss,* I think. *Just put a pillow under my head, set the drainage system beside the bed, and leave so I can tell my parents goodbye and die.*

"What the hell is going on? Where am I?" I ask, my voice raspy from the intubation.

Their conversation abruptly stops. "Hey, Mr. Bowen. You're at Pitt County Memorial Hospital on the neurosurgical floor. My name is Dr. Turner. I'm a pulmonologist here, and this is Dr. Hardy, the neurosurgeon who removed your vest so I could insert a chest tube." Dr. Turner tells me they have placed me in a kinetic bed to keep my lungs from filling up with fluid.

The third man, a representative for the company that sells the bed, proudly states, "That's right. This bed turns 270 degrees, twenty-four hours a day to help prevent pneumonia," as if the bed's capabilities should impress me.

Dr. Turner adds that the bed will help clear up the fluid around my lung, and it does an excellent job of preventing bedsores.

THE VIEWFINDER

When the dialogue stops, the bed rep inserts pads that secure my head and neck. Dr. Hardy oversees the placement of these pads, making sure they don't interfere with the pins screwed into my skull. Next, he places large pads on the insides and outsides of both my arms.

Before the rep places pads against my torso, Dr. Turner asks him to put an additional pad above and below where my chest tube exits my side to create a space so that the hose can drain properly. However, the representative is hesitant to follow Dr. Turner's recommendation because he has a specific protocol to follow when setting up the bed. Dr. Turner assures the rep that his request supersedes the company's protocol.

After putting the chest pads in place, the representative inserts pads along the inside and outside of my legs. To add to my confinement, my neck is once again placed in traction. Several large straps resembling seat belts stretch across the bed to hold me in place. With the flip of a switch, the bed slowly rotates, and I realize my hell on earth has reached a new level.

It's close to one o'clock in the morning when the bed rep leaves. Dr. Hardy tells my parents he'll be by in the morning during rounds to check on me. Dr. Turner informs them that he has ordered additional blood work and placed me on meds to combat the pulmonary embolism, pleurisy, and pneumonia in my right lung. Mama and Daddy follow the doctors to the door and thank them for taking such good care of me.

When I'm finally alone with my parents, I'm too emotionally drained to even

CHAPTER 5

shed a tear. The depth of despair I feel is unfathomable. As the bed rotates toward them, I say, "I love you guys very much, but I'm tired of living like this."

Mama leans over and, without so much as a hitch in her voice, says, "We love you too, honey. It's going to be okay. You get some rest."

Upset, Daddy quickly turns away and walks out of the room. He knows I'm saying goodbye, that I'm giving up. Perhaps it's father's intuition.

Why have I waited until now, on my deathbed, to utter those three words? There are countless times I've had the chance to say I love you, but I squandered them away. I can never get those times back. I close my eyes and say a simple prayer: *Lord, I'm tired. I am tired of fighting, tired of living like this. I pray you take my life right now. If it's not my time, then bless me with a quality of life that I can live with. Give me a purpose in life.* This prayer brings me some peace. As I drift off to sleep, I truly believe I've seen my parents for the last time.

CHAPTER 6

NOT LONG AFTER my prayer, Daddy races back into the room and over to my bed. His eyes are bloodshot from crying. With his voice faltering, he says, "Son, I love you with all my heart. We've come a long way, and we are *not* giving up now!"

My father's words comfort me as I fall asleep, but I still don't know if I'll wake up again. During the night, the viewfinder produces a vivid image. This time, it's not from my past but a glimpse into the future.

In the image, I see myself lying on a large wooden table covered with a padded, dark green mat. A set of chrome parallel bars stand near the table. I immediately recognize the outfit I'm wearing: a fluorescent yellow, long-sleeved shirt, black spandex tights, and my navy blue Nike running shoes. Ironically, it's the exact thing I was wearing the night before my accident when my teammate Pagano and I went for a run.

I'm lying on my back with my knees bent and my arms across my chest. A female physical therapist is holding my feet as if I'm getting ready to knock out

CHAPTER 6

a set of sit-ups. We're both smiling, and I'm free of that torturous halo and vest. On my left wrist, I'm wearing a gold ID bracelet. Although I can't see the bracelet that clearly, I know it has the date of my accident and the date of my release from rehab inscribed on it. The letters *WJB*, *BPB*, *WLB*, and *SMC* are engraved on the underside of the bracelet; they're the initials of my dad, mom, brother, and Sharon. This image of me shows a happy and hopeful young man.

At noon the following day, I wake up from what my parents describe as twelve hours of "being dead asleep." Although my condition is still critical, I feel blessed. The viewfinder has provided me with an image—or perhaps a vision—showing me that there are better days ahead, and I feel like God has answered my prayer. He has a purpose for my life, and it's not to simply exist.

When I share my dream with my parents, they seem to read little into it. The last thing they want to do is give me false hope. Even so, they're excited to see me with enthusiasm for the future, which means, at least for now, I'm not giving up. I look at my parents standing side by side and feel a depth of gratitude for them that did not exist inside my heart twelve hours earlier. The only explanation I have for this metamorphosis of the heart is that a spiritual intervention occurred while I was sleeping. From this day forward, all I want to do is make them proud of me.

Waking up on the rotating kinetic bed is an odd sensation, and I'll have to get acclimated to the constant turning. Out of the corner of my eye, I see an IV drip, and I can hear the drainage system hard at work siphoning fluid from my chest. Suddenly, it all comes back to me: waking up in the rehab gasping for air, the intubation, and the insertion of the chest tube.

Unbeknownst to me, Dr. Turner and Dr. Hardy were both already in to see me this morning. Apparently, my dad—needing someone to blame for my condition—gave Dr. Turner a stern talking-to. That I have taken a turn for the worse has left Daddy's trust in doctors at an all-time low. He believes my life is hanging in the balance because the powers that be at New Hanover Regional Medical Center discharged me too soon. He wants assurance from Dr. Turner that he won't send me back over to the rehabilitation center until I fully recover from the pneumonia and the blood clot in my lung dissolves.

Dr. Turner is sympathetic to my dad's frustration about my premature release from the hospital in Wilmington, even if for no other reason than to redirect my father's attention to my present situation. Dr. Turner is a straight shooter. He's honest with my parents and tells them that I'm very sick. He says a pulmonary embolism can be life-threatening, so his main priorities right now are to make sure the blood-thinning medicine is working and that I don't develop additional complications. He assures my parents that I'm in excellent hands, and they are doing everything possible to give me the best chance for recovery. Dr. Turner promises Daddy he will only discharge me when I'm well and not a moment before.

Another blessing that has developed during my twelve-hour period of transformation is that I'm no longer craving Demerol. I still have pain in my neck and chest as well as muscle spasms, but I'm no longer experiencing symptoms from the

CHAPTER 6

withdrawal of Demerol. Score another point for the Lord. And by midafternoon, I'm already getting accustomed to the constant movement of the rotating bed.

Not having slept much in the past twelve hours, my parents are both napping when a nurse named Charles quietly enters my room.

"Hey, my man, what's happenin'?" he says. "My name's Charles. I'll be cathin' you in the daytime." He's soft-spoken with a pencil-thin mustache and porcelain white teeth, and to me he looks like a dead ringer for Billy Dee Williams. He reaches down and flips a switch that stops my bed from rotating.

"You'll be doing what in the daytime?" I ask, perplexed.

"You got a Foley catheter in your bladder, prob'ly been there since you got injured. I'm here to take it out. From now on, you'll in-and-out cath, which means I'll put a catheter in your bladder, empty your bladder, then take the catheter out."

As he prepares to take out the catheter, I look away and I brace myself for a painful spasm.

"Hey, man, how'd you get hurt?" he asks.

"Car accident," I reply.

"Dang. Sorry to hear 'bout that, brother. Your fault?"

"I'm afraid so," I say.

"Anybody else in the car?"

"No, just me."

"That's one good thing. . . . All done, my brother. I'll see you in about five hours," he says while making a few check marks in his paperwork.

"You're done already?" I say, relieved that it didn't cause a spasm.

Charles smiles and says, "Man, I'm the best in the business! You know what they say: it ain't braggin' when it's true."

I chuckle at his remarks and feel a slight spasm when the chest tube moves inside me, but it feels good to laugh. First impressions are important to me, and I immediately like Charles.

My laughing wakes Daddy from his nap just in time to introduce himself to Charles before he leaves. I tell Daddy the Foley catheter has been removed, and from now on, I'll be cathed several times a day. While I view it as a positive development, my dad only sees it as an additional source of pain for his son.

When dinnertime rolls around, for the first time in weeks, I'm hungry—but not for hospital food. Instead, I'm craving a Wendy's chicken sandwich. The fast-food restaurant is just down the street from the hospital, and Daddy is happy to get it for me. I eat most of the sandwich, but strangely, the soda tastes too sweet to me. This seems odd to me because before my accident, I had at least one soft drink a day.

It's unnecessary for both of my parents to stay the night, so Mama decides to stay tonight. When Charles shows up just before seven to catheterize me, it's the perfect time for Daddy to leave so he can avoid seeing a fourteen-inch tube entering my private parts. Although he's reluctant to leave me, he knows I'm in excellent hands with Mama here.

Once Daddy leaves, Charles caths me. The process is a piece of cake compared to having an intubation tube stuck down my throat twenty-four hours earlier.

CHAPTER 6

Before he leaves, Charles lets me know that James will do the honors tonight and in the morning.

My second night on the rotating kinetic bed is a far cry from the blissful sleep I got the night before. Whenever I'm asleep and the bed rotates from one side to the other, I feel like I'm falling and abruptly wake up. At midnight, I'm still awake. To compound the problem, whenever my weight is shifted to the right side, my chest aches. I get a reprieve from the pain when James shows up to cath me. I don't hear him come into the room; I just notice the bed stop moving. "Thank you, Jesus," I say out loud.

"I'm not Jesus, I'm James. You must be Mike," he says giggling.

I open my eyes. "Hey, James. You're a godsend for stopping this bed," I reply. "Charles said you'd be coming by tonight."

"Was he talkin' bad about me?" James jokingly asks.

"No."

"I bet he told you he's the best cath man in the business," James says.

"Yep, he sure did!" I reply with a chuckle. "Said it's not braggin' if it's true!"

"Don't listen to that fool. He knows *I'm* the best."

When I hear James put on his gloves, I wait for the bright fluorescent light above my bed to come on, but instead I hear a package open and then the sound of urine landing in the bottom of a urinal. I think to myself, *This guy is a magician. He's taking care of my business in the dark! Wait 'til I tell Charles about James's stealth abilities.*

Before he leaves, James reaches down to flip the ON button to my bed.

"Hey, James, I'll pay you twenty bucks not to flip that switch," I implore.

"Sorry, brother. No can do," he says in a sympathetic voice. "You know these new beds are lifesavers."

"Maybe so, but it's killing the right side of my chest."

Before James leaves, he tells me he'll see me around six. With his departure, I mentally prepare myself for five more sleepless hours of rotating side to side. But out of my torment comes a tremendous blessing: during one of the many times I wake up from experiencing the sensation of falling, I feel my arms move to break my fall.

"Yes!" I shout, waking up my mom.

She springs out of the recliner. "Michael, what's wrong?"

"I think I just moved my arms!"

Mama turns on the light and stands by my bed while I unsuccessfully try to reproduce the movement. I tell Mama the movement was barely perceptible, but it wasn't a spasm. I know I'm not imagining it. It's the wee hours of the morning, so I tell her to go back to sleep. Then I spend the next few hours visualizing my arms moving; it's my best effort at some form of telepathic exercise. However, my visualization technique is fruitless.

James shows up a little before six. I'm surprised to see that my mother is up and reading her book. James introduces himself to her and gets right to work, grabbing a pair of latex gloves and a sterile catheter from his cart and placing them

CHAPTER 6

between my legs. Then he reaches for the plastic urinal hanging on the bed rail. As he goes to grab it, he misjudges the distance and the lightweight urinal slides down the rail toward the floor. James reacts quickly and swoops it up in his hand. Watching his reaction gives me an idea.

"James, do me a favor before you cath me?" I ask.

"Sure, brother, what can I help you with?" he responds.

"Raise the head of my bed just a little, please," I reply. Then I add, "Mama, will you come stand by my bed and watch my left arm? And James, on the count of three, I want you to toss the urinal toward my left hand."

"With the lid on or off?" he asks with a mischievous grin.

"On," I laugh.

On three, he tosses the urinal in my direction. My eyes track the urinal like a tennis ball leaving my opponent's racket. I feel my left arm and hand twitch as I reach for the urinal. The urinal lands beside my arm, but Mama and James cheer in unison, acknowledging that they saw my arm move. Mama leans over the bed and tells me, "Your daddy is going to be so excited when he hears the good news!"

After several seconds of hoopla, James gets down to the business of catheterizing me while my mom heads to the cafeteria for some breakfast. A little after seven, a nurse shows up to change out an IV bag. I ask her if there's anything she can do about the padding against the right side of my chest because it's too tight. I tell her that muscle spasms in my chest kept me up most of the night. She leaves the room and returns several minutes later with another nurse. The two of them loosen the pad lining my torso on the right side. But to keep me secure in the bed, they tighten the pads around my right arm and leg. The plan works, and the pain in the right side of my chest decreases enough to stop the spasms. As a result, during my third and fourth nights in the rotating bed, I sleep in relative comfort. I only wake up occasionally when my body weight shifts from one side to the other.

However, on the morning of December 9, the luxury of pain-free sleep comes to a screeching halt. While receiving a sponge bath from two nurses, an unfamiliar woman dressed in a business suit walks into my room, peeks inside the curtain, sees me, and abruptly leaves. To bathe me, the nurses turn off the kinetic bed, unbuckle the bed straps, and loosen the padding. To me, the few minutes of untethered freedom are priceless. No sooner do the nurses finish bathing me and leave my room when the unfamiliar woman returns with the head nurse.

The head nurse gets an earful from this woman, but I only catch the tail end of the conversation: "If DHHS finds out the guidelines for these new kinetic beds are not being followed, the hospital can lose its bed license!" she says emphatically. "Patients are to be secure in these beds at all times unless it's a medical emergency!"

As I listen, I'm thinking, *Why is this woman, who is not a nurse, hell-bent on making sure the straps and pads are secure when the bed is in the off position? I'm paralyzed! Where am I going?* Then I realize that this woman is another bed rep.

When she finishes giving the head nurse a verbal tongue-lashing, the bed rep adjusts the pads and straps on my bed. With displaced aggression, she begins by tightening the two pads that line the sides of my face. She pulls them so tight

CHAPTER 6

I can feel my pulse pounding inside my head. Then she readjusts the arm pads that line my torso. During her inspection, she notices the additional soft padding wedged against the right side of my chest, which was placed there at the request of Dr. Turner. She removes it, shakes her head in disgust, and says, "It's a miracle you haven't fallen out of the bed!"

"Dr. Turner put the added padding there to protect my chest tube," I tell her.

She ignores my comment and tightens the torso pads anyway. When she does, the pad on the right side pushes the chest tube further inside my chest cavity, triggering excruciating spasms in both legs. I scream in pain, but the bed rep is unfazed by my yelp or the violent jerking of my legs. The head nurse steps forward as if getting ready to say something, but then she stops. After tightening the pads that keep my legs secure, the bed rep flips the switch and starts the bed rotating, then the two of them leave the room.

The confinement of the pads coupled with severe neck and chest pain produces a rage inside me that I unleash on the next person who walks into the room. I unload on a junior nurse, screaming, "You better get that bitch back in here right now to loosen these goddamn pads!" My verbal assault stuns the nurse as it echoes down the hallway. Hearing my rant, another nurse rushes in.

Continuing with my diatribe, I bellow, "All I want to do is walk again, and all you freakin' people want to do is keep me pinned to this torture chamber!" With all the strength I can muster in my neck and left arm, I fight against my entrapment. Surprisingly, my tirade reveals my ability to raise my left arm enough

THE VIEWFINDER

to make contact with the strap that's three to four inches above it.

One of the nurses steps forward, grabs my chin and forehead, and yells, "Stop moving your neck!" Then she tells the other nurse to stop the bed. The other nurse hits the off switch and my call button to ask for backup.

Returning from breakfast, my mother hears the commotion from down the hall and hurries into the room just in time to see the two nurses pleading for me to settle down. As Mama comes into my line of sight, my fury quickly dissipates into tears. The nurse removes her hands from my face and steps back so Mama can be at my bedside. Over and over, I tell her all I want to do is learn to walk again.

While comforting me, she turns and addresses the nurses. "Why is he so upset? What happened?" She glances back at me then glares at the two of them.

They look at each other dumbfounded. Attempting to explain, one nurse says, "He's complaining that the pads on his bed are too tight, but I don't know why!"

Responding to the distress call, the head nurse scurries into the room. Panting, she asks, "What's going on?"

One nurse begins to say, "He's complaining that—"

But my mother interrupts her, saying, "My son is not a complainer. If he says the pads are too tight, then they're too tight."

The head nurse's chin drops to her chest. She immediately realizes what has happened and explains to my mom what transpired earlier with the representative from the bed company. Before the nurse leaves the room, my mother gives her formidable instructions to immediately contact Dr. Turner and Dr. Hardy and have them

CHAPTER 6

assess the setup of the bed. An hour later, Dr. Turner's physician's assistant shows up to make sure my chest tube is draining properly. He reapplies the soft padding around the chest tube and loosens the pad that runs along the right side of my chest.

While making his evening rounds, Dr. Hardy walks directly to the foot of my bed and shuts it off. He checks the padding against my head and neck and, with some colorful language, readjusts the pads. Then he makes sure my morning tantrum didn't loosen the pins screwed into my skull. When he finishes his inspection, he leans over the bed railing, looks at me, and says, "There will be no more moving your head and neck, understood?" As he walks past Mama and Daddy, he adds, "There will be no more bed nazis stopping by either."

○ ○ ○

After a week in the kinetic bed, my condition improves from critical to serious. Eventually, Dr. Turner upgrades my condition to stable when X-rays show my right lung is clear enough to have the chest tube removed. The scans show that the pneumonia in my lung is clearing up, and blood thinners are dissolving the life-threatening blood clot. In fact, my condition has improved enough that Dr. Hardy has ordered physical therapy for me, and I'm thrilled.

On Thursday, December 12, my physical therapist comes to my room, and we hit it off immediately.

"Hey, Michael! My name is Kim. I'll be your physical therapist while you're in the hospital," she says with a smile. "I hear you're quite the tennis player."

"Don't believe everything you hear," I reply jokingly. "Do you play tennis?"

"No. I tried once, but I couldn't keep the ball in the court," she laughs.

"That makes two of us," I return.

As Kim waits for the bed to rotate to a flat position, she asks me about my family. I describe my humble upbringing. As I do, I observe her facial expressions. *Is she really listening to me or just waiting for me to stop talking so she can talk?* Her expressive smile and green eyes suggest a strong sense of compassion for others.

As she removes the large bed straps, I have time to inquire about her family. She's a single mother and has a two-year-old daughter.

With the bed in the off position and my straps removed, Kim begins a thorough physical evaluation, scoring the strength and movement of my limbs. She starts with my right arm and hand, which are both still paralyzed. When she grabs my arm, I want desperately to feel her touch, but I don't. The lack of sensation is the result of damage to my peripheral nervous system. On her clipboard, she documents the lack of movement and feeling.

Next, she asks me to move my right leg. As hard as I try, it's a futile effort. I cannot move my right foot or any of my toes. However, when Kim holds up my left arm and asks me to move my fingers, I can move each one on command. When she asks me to bend my left elbow, I raise my arm off the bed six inches or more—twice as high than when I had my emotional meltdown with the nurses a few days ago. Even better news is seeing my triceps extend my left arm a couple inches. The highlight of this evaluation is the slight movement in my left leg, foot, and toes. As Kim scores the strength in my leg, she acknowledges

CHAPTER 6

these movements are all good signs of things to come.

After the evaluation, she manipulates my arms and legs through a series of range-of-motion exercises, and I notice her hands are strong but feminine at the same time. With mixed emotions, I watch her move my limbs. Although I'm excited about the progress that the left side of my body is making, I'm concerned that I may not regain the ability to use my right arm or leg.

During our session, Kim makes me feel like I'm her only patient. She mentions that therapists who work in the rehab center love to work with athletes because they have a strong work ethic. Whether intentional or not, she says just the right things to keep my vulnerable self-esteem intact.

"So, besides being a tennis pro, is there anything else I should know about you?" she asks.

"Well, I'm also a movie star, if you must know," I respond playfully. Then I tell Kim all about my movie debut.

She just smiles and shakes her head in disbelief as I tell her what happened before, during, and after my accident.

As I'm sharing my story, my parents walk in and introduce themselves to Kim. They make polite conversation while Kim straps me back into the bed and it starts rotating once again. As she's leaving, my parents follow her into the hallway, and I eavesdrop on their conversation. Kim explains to my parents that athletes with spinal injuries can be susceptible to bouts of depression and extreme mood changes if their physical limitations become too much for them to bear. When

THE VIEWFINDER

Mama describes my meltdown with the nursing staff a few days earlier, Kim tells her that such behavior is not uncommon.

By mid-December, I have settled into a daily regimen. I eat three meals a day, have regular visits from Charles and James who tend to my bladder, and the nurses take care of my bowel needs. The area where the steel screws enter my skin is cleaned daily to prevent infection, and occasionally I get a chest X-ray and bloodwork. To exercise my lungs, I spend five to ten minutes each morning and evening blowing into a spirometer.

Just as important, every day the nurses check my body for bedsores. Even though the rotating kinetic bed helps prevent pressure sores, the nurses vigilantly look for tender spots around my shoulder blades, hips, and ankles. I've lost a significant amount of muscle and fat—the two tissues that provide a cushion for the skin—so I'm at risk for developing pressure sores. Kim has warned me that a bedsore can derail physical therapy, and the highlight of my week is the days I work with her. Besides being my physical therapist, she has become somewhat of a psychotherapist to me. During our sessions, she helps me paint a mental picture of what the future will look like once I'm moved back over to the rehab center and am finally free of the physical and mental trappings of the rotating kinetic bed.

By my fifteenth day on the neurosurgical floor, I'm weary of the constant turning of the kinetic bed. Every night before I drift off to sleep, I pray that the Lord

CHAPTER 6

will give me the mental fortitude to make it through another day. All signs point to my recovery: the blood clot has dissolved, my latest X-rays show no pneumonia, and my right lung is clear of fluid. In fact, by this time, I've been stable for over a week. However, my eagerness to free myself from my rotating torture chamber is no match for my father's determination to keep me in it until Dr. Turner believes it's safe to move me back over to the rehab center.

I'm surprised to find out from a nurse that Dr. Turner has cleared me to transfer back down to the rehab center, but it's Dr. Hardy who is hesitant to release me! For the past two days when Dr. Hardy has shown up for rounds, I've asked him when I'm getting out of here. To my frustration, he keeps telling me not yet. Now, Dr. Hardy is not a man to argue with. Although he's short in stature (only a few inches over five feet), he's a revered neurosurgeon. And it's hard to argue with a neurosurgeon who's had his own devastating injury. While carving a turkey, Dr. Hardy cut and severed a tendon in his hand, which ended his career as a surgeon. So he decided to go to law school. While he was there, he found a neurosurgeon who was doing cutting-edge surgeries to transplant tendons from the leg to the hand. Dr. Hardy's surgery was a success, and after many hours of occupational therapy, he regained his ability to operate as a neurosurgeon. If that's not an inspiring story, I don't know what is.

On the evening of Friday, December 20, my parents, Lee, Sharon, and I can hear Dr. Hardy, his two PAs, and a small entourage of medical students making their way from room to room visiting patients. To be clear, it's only Dr. Hardy's voice we hear alongside the clickety-clack of everyone else's footsteps. Like E. F. Hutton, when Dr. Hardy speaks, everybody listens.

When the group enters my room, Dr. Hardy greets us while one of his PAs reads through my medical chart. I notice the interns immediately begin writing in their notepads.

As Dr. Hardy walks over to me, I mentally prepare for our customary exchange: He'll ask me how I'm feeling. I'll tell him I feel good enough to get out of this bed. Then he'll respond that he can see I'm feeling better, but he doesn't think I'm ready yet.

"Michael, how are you feeling today?" he asks.

"I'm ready to get out of this bed," I reply.

I wait to hear him say, "I know you are," but instead, Dr. Hardy moves to the foot of my bed and shuts it off. Then he leans over the bed rail and says, "You've come a long way, son. Two weeks ago, you had one leg in the bed and two feet in the grave!" he chuckles. He backs away from the bed, grabs my medical chart from his PA, and scribbles something on it. Turning to my parents, he says, "I'll be by first thing Monday morning to put his vest back on. Rehab services will come for him soon afterward." He then leans down and flips the ON switch to my bed, looks at me, winks, and says, "You guys enjoy your weekend," as he leads his entourage out of the room.

Once the room clears, Daddy comes over to my bed. We say nothing; we just exchange smiles as he smooths my hair to one side with his hand. It's with

CHAPTER 6

tremendous relief that I realize my fifteen days of being confined to a bed that seldom stops moving will finally come to a halt on Monday morning.

At this point, it seems that I have weathered the storm of setbacks. On the night of December 5, I wanted my life to end. Now it's five days before Christmas, and I can't wait to begin a new chapter in my life and start rebuilding my body. Deep down inside, I know a higher power has made this possible; God has blessed me and my family. I also believe the mental and physical anguish I've endured and overcome in the past month have prepared me for whatever lies ahead.

On the night of Sunday, December 22, we have a quiet celebration to mark my impending return to rehab. As an early Christmas gift, the head nurse has even given the okay for the kinetic bed to stop turning for an hour, so I celebrate with a big bag of peanut M&M's, my favorite.

The CCU, which is adjacent to the neurosurgical floor, is full of seriously ill patients, but tonight, I'm not one of them. My parents and I have grown accustomed to hearing "Code Blue" announced over the loudspeaker accompanied by the sounds of running footsteps and then wailing family members. On this night, we only hear a few carolers walking door-to-door singing Christmas songs. Hearing their harmonious voices, I reminisce as I nostalgically recall attending Christmas Eve services with Gramma and listening to our church choir sing those timeless songs.

When we hear "Silent Night" echoing in the hallway, Lee walks to the door and gestures for the choir to come into my room. As Sharon sits on the side of the bed and my parents relax in the two recliners, we sing along with the choir.

I know it'll become another one of those moments etched into my mind for the rest of my life. Overcome with emotion, a steady stream of tears flows down my cheeks. I can't help thinking how good it feels to cry happy tears instead of tears brought on by pain and sickness.

When the choir finishes singing, Daddy walks over to the bed. Brushing my hair to the side, he says, "Having you out of this bed and heading down to the rehab center is the best Christmas present you could give your mother and me."

"Speaking of Christmas," Mama adds, "have you given any thought about what you might want for Christmas?"

"Yes, I have," I quickly respond. "I want the gold bracelet I saw myself wearing in my dream." Although I haven't told anyone, I believe re-creating the details I saw in that vision is the key to attaining my greatest wish: walking again.

CHAPTER 7

THE MONDAY MORNING move from the hospital down to the rehabilitation center can't come soon enough. My parents are at the hospital by eight, waiting on Dr. Hardy. In the meantime, Kim stops by to give me the news that she'll continue to be my therapist when I'm back over at the rehab center. That's great news for two reasons: one, I feel we have a good chemistry between us; and two, in my vision, I saw myself lying on a padded table working with a female therapist. I desperately want my dream to become a reality, and that reality starts with Kim. I create a motto to live by while I'm in rehab: "All day long, do your very best, and let God worry about the rest."

As promised, Dr. Hardy shows up a little before nine to put my vest back on and secure the rods to my halo. Before he leaves, he wishes us good luck.

After that, I'm transferred out of the kinetic bed and onto a gurney. Once I'm out of the bed, I get a bird's-eye view of the contraption, which is a monstrous work of art. As much as I'd like to douse it with gasoline and set it on fire, I know it probably helped save my life.

THE VIEWFINDER

My return trip to the rehab center is much more enjoyable than the fast-paced sprint I experienced when I left it a few weeks ago. I get an eerie feeling, though, because the orderlies place me in the same room where I almost lost my life. For a second time, Mama and Daddy unpack my clothes, a growing collection of get-well cards, and my stuffed lion, Arnold.

As I settle into my room, an older guy comes through the door in his wheelchair. At first glance, he looks like Neil Young—yes, *that* Neil Young. Long muttonchops hang down from his applejack hat, and his big smile is contagious. While I'm expecting him to break into some rendition of "Ohio" or "Old Man," Daddy steps forward and introduces himself. "Hi, I'm Bo Bowen, and this is my son, Mackel" (his affectionate pronunciation of Michael), he says, pointing to me.

Neil Young's doppelganger replies, "Mike Hamer."

My dad extends his hand. As he does, Mike struggles but manages to reach out with his paralyzed hand and place it in my dad's. As is his custom, my dad tests Mike's sense of humor with a few of his best jokes and has him chuckling in no time. Watching Mike's face as he interacts with my parents, I can see that paralysis has done nothing to diminish what appears to be a radiant personality.

"How long have you been here, Mike?" Mama asks.

"About two weeks," he replies.

Finally, Daddy's curiosity gets the best of him. "So, Mike, how'd you get injured?" he casually inquires.

"Do you guys live around here?" Mike asks.

CHAPTER 7

"Yes, we live in Washington Park," Daddy responds.

"So you're familiar with Whichard's Beach, just outside of Washington?"

"Oh yeah . . . been there many times," I say, joining the conversation.

"Well, while my friends and I were swimming down at Whichard's Beach, I dove into shallow water, hit my head on the riverbed, and hyperextended my neck, injuring my spinal cord," Mike explains.

Mike tells us he's an incomplete quadriplegic, and he can't move or feel anything below his chest, but he's thankful to have some movement in his arms. Hearing this, I immediately feel guilty for having the ability to move my left arm, hand, and leg, even if it is only slightly.

"How about you, Michael? How'd you hurt yourself?" Mike asks.

"Car accident," I reply, but before I can share my story with Mike, Dr. Alsentzer walks into the room. As my parents reintroduce themselves to the doctor, Mike nods an acknowledgement to Dr. A and wheels his way out of the room.

Dr. A looks at me and says with a touch of sarcasm in his voice, "I hope you're planning to stay with us a little longer than your last visit."

I smile and tell him I hope so too.

He's here to give me a physical evaluation, so my parents step out of the room while he assesses me. He does the pinprick test and several others that Kim performed on me in the hospital during her initial assessment, and he's encouraged by the progress I've made. During the evaluation, I ask Dr. A when I will start physical therapy. When he tells me not until after the Christmas holiday, it's difficult to hide my disappointment because I'm eager to get started. He explains that since I've been lying flat on my back for so long, it could be challenging for me to sustain a healthy blood pressure. So my first goal must be to sit up straight in the bed without passing out.

"That's not much of a goal," I say skeptically.

He glances back at me before leaving the room and says, "For some patients, it is."

By the time lunch arrives, I'm settled into my room. Since visiting hours don't start until five, my parents leave with plans to return later. I tell them there's no need to come back tonight and that I'll see them tomorrow.

I spend the afternoon gradually having the head of my bed raised a few inches every hour. The process is tedious, and I'm bored lying in bed. However, the fact that this bed isn't continuously rotating back and forth, I must acknowledge, is a blessing.

Around four o'clock, Kim knocks on the door and asks with a smile, "How do you like your new bed?"

"I'm a happy camper," I admit.

"I see the nursing staff already has your head elevated," she observes.

When I explain that their goal is to have me sitting up straight by the following morning, she cautiously advises me to take it slow.

During her visit, Kim does a quick assessment to measure my progress. By this time, I can almost make a fist with my left hand, and I can bend my left elbow ninety degrees and raise my arm a foot or more off the bed. I can also wiggle the toes of my left foot and bend my knee about fifteen degrees.

CHAPTER 7

However, except for a tiny bit of movement in the fingers on my right hand, the right side of my body remains paralyzed. Kim tells me I'm making excellent progress, and I pray she's not just telling me this to keep my spirits up. Before she leaves, she reiterates what Dr. A told me: there will be no therapy session on Wednesday since it's Christmas Day.

As nightfall sets in, my thoughts focus on Christmas. I want to get gifts for those close to me, but I know I'll have to depend on my brother to pull off this feat. As if reading my mind, Lee walks into the room.

"Well, this is a surprise. I was just thinking about you. What are you doing here?" I ask.

"I had to come check out your new place, but I see you're in the same room you were before." Then he adds with a grin, "I just saw two cute nurses in the hallway. You did tell them you have an eligible older brother who's twice as good-looking as you, right?"

"Well, I mentioned that I have an older brother," I respond and smile back at him.

"When do you start physical therapy?"

"Not until after Christmas," I reply with a hint of disappointment.

"What?" Lee exclaims in disbelief.

"Yep. First, I have to sit up and transfer to a wheelchair before I can do anything else," I explain. "Hey, speaking of Christmas . . . I need your help buying gifts for Mama, Daddy, and Sharon."

"What are you thinking about getting Sharon?" he asks.

"I don't know . . . maybe a sweater," I answer hesitantly.

Ever the problem solver, Lee says, "I have an idea. We have a Polaroid camera at work. I'll go to the mall and take pictures of some sweaters and whatever you're thinking of getting Mama and Daddy. Then I'll bring the photos to you, and you can pick from them."

"That would be great!"

Just before seven when her shift ends, my daytime nurse stops by one last time to see how I'm adjusting to the small elevation to my bed. I say, "No problems so far," so she raises the head of the bed a few more inches before leaving. Following her departure, Mike Hamer and two of his friends enter the room.

Making introductions, I say, "Mike, this is my brother, Lee."

"Hey, Lee. I'm Mike Hamer, and these are my friends Laura and Sue."

"So, Mike, what do you do for a living?" Lee asks casually as he extends his hand toward the two women.

"I'm a professor of English at East Carolina University and a part-time musician," he responds.

Lee asks Mike about his musical background. Mike tells us that, in his spare time, he, Laura, Sue, and a few others play in a jazz band called the Lemon Sisters and Rutabaga Brothers. Before his accident, Mike was a bass player, but now, with the limited use of his hands and fingers, he's learning to master the hammered dulcimer instead.

CHAPTER 7

Carrying on a conversation with Mike is refreshing because he's very positive and upbeat. It's hard to dwell on negative thoughts when you're around him. *God must know that I need a roommate like him,* I think to myself.

When the conversation starts to wind down, Mike and his bandmates make their way to the other side of the curtain that divides the room. I turn on the television, and ESPN is showing highlights of Sunday's college basketball games. Watching the highlights gives me an idea. "Hey, Lee," I say. "Can you make me a basketball backboard and hoop to put at the foot of my bed?"

"How big?" he asks.

"Four feet by four feet."

Eyeballing the end of the bed, he responds, "No problem. Piece of cake."

Lee pulls his chair up next to my bed, and we watch television until visiting hours are over. Before he leaves, Lee takes another look at the foot of my bed and lets me know that he'll work on the basketball backboard and bring it next time he visits.

It's been a good day but a long one, so I turn out my light around ten. An hour later, I'm still awake. I wonder why, but then I realize that it's because the bed isn't turning! As much as I despised the rotating bed, I've become accustomed to moving back and forth while I sleep. Even so, I'll take the stillness and resulting sleeplessness over the kinetic bed any day of the week.

While I lie awake with my thoughts, I wonder what it'll feel like when I'm sitting straight up in bed. I see myself shooting Nerf balls at the hoop and backboard

THE VIEWFINDER

Lee is going to make for me. I'm still awake at one o'clock in the morning when I notice a familiar face quietly enter the room. "My man, James. What's happening, brother?" I say.

Surprised by my greeting, he asks, "Why you still awake?"

"You won't believe this, but I can't sleep because the bed isn't turning!"

"I can go get that kinetic bed and bring it down here if ya want," he says sarcastically.

With a chuckle, I respond, "Don't you dare!"

It's Christmas Eve morning, and I'm up early. The sun is peeking through the window of our room, and although I'm sleep-deprived, I'm excited. For thirty-five days, I've been lying flat on my back, and I am so ready to get out of bed and sit in a chair.

At seven thirty, I hear the breakfast cart making its rounds. I'm now on a soft protein diet to help me gain weight. On the day of my accident, I weighed 165 pounds and had about 6 percent body fat. Looking at myself now, I'm sure I don't weigh more than a buck forty, and it's a depressing realization.

My first breakfast in rehab presents me with the challenge of feeding myself. Until now, my mom, Sharon, or a nurse has helped feed me. But with my breakfast sitting in front of me, I'm making a mess as I unsuccessfully try to load a mouthful of scrambled eggs onto a fork. I do, however, securely harpoon the sausage links and polish them off. Unfortunately, when I try my hand at

CHAPTER 7

spooning grits into my mouth, most of it ends up down the inside of my vest. When I finish eating, my chest is a debris field of eggs and grits. There's nothing like the aroma of eggs and grits mixed with sweat seeping into your nostrils with every breath you take!

Once I finish my breakfast, two nurses stop in and introduce themselves as Sharon and Althea. I recognize something familiar in Althea's voice during her introduction and realize that her heavy southern drawl reminds me of the TV character Mama, aka Thelma Harper, on the sitcom *Mama's Family*. On the show, Vicki Lawrence plays Thelma, a buxom, gray-haired, outspoken southern woman who is set in her ways.

As Althea works to clean me up—which is quite a challenge because of the fishing expedition needed to retrieve food from inside my vest—she seems a bit agitated having to perform this task. Sharon puts on gloves, opens a packet of Betadine, and cleans the area where the pins screw into my skull. Afterward, she and Althea work in unison to turn me on my side and insert a suppository then lay me back down on a metal bedpan. Believe me when I say that it's a humbling experience having someone else take care of your bowel needs.

After a successful bowel movement, Althea wipes my backside and prepares to give me a sponge bath. As she goes to grab a clean hospital gown off her cart, I ask her to dress me in my workout clothes rather than a hospital gown.

"Sweetie," she says, "you will *not* be workin' out today. Your workout's gonna be sittin' up in this bed without passin' out."

"But I *will* need my clothes on when I'm transferred to my wheelchair later today," I object.

"That's not necessarily gonna happen today."

"In my mind, I've already accomplished today's goal of sitting up in bed," I sternly explain. "So I need to see myself in my workout clothes with my running shoes on!"

"You want us to put your sneakers on you in bed even though you ain't gettin' out of bed today?" she utters in disbelief.

"That's right," I confirm.

Althea sighs heavily and rolls her eyes. Even so, she asks me where my clothes are. After I tell her, she gets them out and tosses a long-sleeved T-shirt and my spandex running tights on the bed. It takes both her and Nurse Sharon to maneuver the tights up my legs and around my waist.

Once my pants are on, Althea looks at my shirt and smugly tells me that it won't fit over my halo. I politely ask her to cut out the neck of my shirt so it'll fit.

"Sure," she grumbles with a heavy dose of contempt, "'cause we ain't got enough to do this mornin'." Then she leaves the room to retrieve a pair of scissors.

I smile at Sharon to break the tension in the room. "Hi, I'm Michael, Althea's archnemesis," I say with a smile.

Sharon chuckles and says, "You know, you and I share the same last name."

"Is that right? I guess I won't have any trouble remembering your name then because my girlfriend's name is Sharon. I'll introduce you to her sometime."

CHAPTER 7

Althea returns with scissors in hand and attacks the neck of my shirt. I don't expect either of them to understand why I'm so adamant about getting dressed. But to me, this is the first time in over a month that I'm wearing clothes, so in my mind, I'm one baby step closer to moving my arms and legs.

By ten in the morning, my bed is almost at a forty-five-degree angle, and I'm loving life. With my left hand, I push the call button and summon Althea to the room.

"Can you bring me a wheelchair?" I ask.

"No, I can't," she responds curtly.

"Why not?"

"'Cause Dr. A says you ain't ready," she barks back.

"So I've got to sit here all day when I could be up and about?" I protest.

Losing her patience, Althea grabs the controls to my bed and starts elevating me to an upright position. She stops the bed just short of ninety degrees, and I immediately feel the weight of the halo, rods, and vest resting on my shoulders. Within seconds, I feel dizzy and short of breath. Cold beads of sweat form on my forehead. Althea glares at me, lowers the bed flat, and elevates my feet. She takes my blood pressure; it's seventy-six over fifty-two, which is quite low.

"Do you still want that wheelchair?" she snaps, leaning over the bed rail to look me in the eye.

"Not right now," I reply dejectedly as I close my eyes and sigh deeply.

"Wise choice," she mumbles. "Once you get some color back in your face, I'll elevate your head a little."

After Althea leaves the room, I spend the rest of the morning lying in bed, choking on the rather large piece of humble pie she has shoved in my mouth. I'm disappointed to have to spend another day in bed, but at least now I understand why it's necessary. I divide my time between watching television, eating lunch, and reading. By late afternoon, Althea has gradually raised the head of my bed back to its previous elevation of forty-five degrees.

Four o'clock arrives, and so does Lee. Although visiting hours are still an hour away, he's managed to sneak a large basketball backboard made of thick cardboard with a Nerf hoop attached to it by the nurses station. He's also been window-shopping at the mall for Christmas gifts. With a few pieces of wire that he brought with him, he attaches the backboard to the base of the bed.

"Whatcha think?" he asks.

"It's awesome! I love it! Thank you so much!"

He pulls two Nerf basketballs out of his jacket, and we play a spirited game of H-O-R-S-E. Afterward, Lee shows me half a dozen Polaroid pictures of sweaters in a variety of colors. I pick out a sweater I think Sharon will like along with a flannel shirt for Daddy and a pair of earrings for Mama. Since it's Christmas Eve, Lee leaves for the mall to buy my last-minute gifts and tells me he'll see me in the morning.

My parents show up a little after seven, pleasantly surprised to see me sitting up for the first time. I'm excited because they stopped by Wendy's and bought me my favorites: a chicken sandwich, fries, and a Frosty. After dinner, the three

CHAPTER 7

of us settle in and watch *Miracle on 34th Street*. Before my parents get ready to leave, Mama kisses me on the forehead and Daddy combs my hair to one side a few times with his fingers.

"You've come along way, baby," Daddy says, reciting another of his favorite sayings. "We'll be here first thing in the morning to spend Christmas together. Gramma's coming too."

With Mike in his bed and me in mine, I can't help but envy those who are spending Christmas Eve at parties and family get-togethers. However, I refuse to allow these feelings of self-pity to linger as I remind myself that I'm fortunate to be celebrating Christmas at all.

THE VIEWFINDER

CHAPTER 8

"Merry Christmas," Daddy says as he escorts Gramma into the room. My grandmother is impeccably dressed, as usual. Wearing a perfectly coordinated pantsuit, blouse, and silk scarf, she reminds me of royalty. As she delicately holds her purse in the crook of her elbow, the image is complete.

Although my father has kept Gramma up-to-date on my progress, I can tell that her first sight of me is alarming. I'm sure the culprit is the set of stainless steel pins sticking out of my skull. When she approaches my bed, she reaches down and grabs my left hand with her tiny hands and places it on the bed rail. To my grandmother, I'm still that little boy sitting beside her on the church pew, receiving the love of Jesus through her prayerful hands. Gramma's eyes shift from our coupled hands back to my face. Again, she focuses on the halo and vest and gets upset.

"It's okay, Gramma. It looks a lot more painful than it is," I say, trying to assure her.

CHAPTER 8

Letting go of my hand, she reaches into her purse and pulls out a check. "Michael, I'm giving you money for Christmas. I want you to sign your name on the back of this check," she says in an authoritative voice.

Before I can respond, Daddy interjects. "Mama, he can't write his name just yet."

"Yes, he can!" she counters, looking at me.

Standing behind Gramma, my father gently places his hands on her shoulders, leans forward, and reminds her that it's Christmas morning. It's not the time to be getting upset, he tells her, it's a celebratory time. Then Daddy reaches down into a bag of Christmas presents and hands her a small gift box to give to me. While I wrestle with the wrapping paper, my father continues to console Gramma.

Seeing my struggle with the gift, Lee helps me open the box. Inside is a gold bracelet, just like I asked for, with the date of my accident engraved on the left side and a blank space on the right. The underside has the initials of Daddy, Mama, Lee, and Sharon. When I tell my grandmother about my vision and how it included a bracelet like this one, she proudly states that the Bowens and her side of the family, the Alligoods, have been visionaries for generations. Whether I'm a clairvoyant or just a man with a vivid imagination, I believe that wearing the bracelet is a significant element in bringing my dream of walking again to fruition.

While we spend the morning opening gifts, some of Mike's bandmates drop by to see him and exchange a few Christmas presents. Daddy can see what my brother and I felt when we first met Mike: there's an aura around him that hasn't allowed the heartbreak of paralysis to diminish his spirit. One of Mike's friends gives him a harmonica, so my family and I are privy to some a cappella singing by the band as Mike plays a few notes on his new instrument. By lunchtime, Gramma, at age eighty-three, has grown tired, so it's time to get her home. Before the family leaves, I promise my grandmother to work extra hard in occupational therapy so I can soon sign my name to that check.

Around two o'clock, Sharon shows up with Christmas gifts in hand. She'd spent the morning with her family in Vanceboro, a half-hour drive from Greenville. Now that she's on winter break from UNC–Wilmington, we're looking forward to spending some quality time together. Since my accident, we've grown closer, and I feel myself falling in love with her. But I haven't told her so out of fear that she won't say it back. My accident not only rendered a blow to my spinal cord but also to my self-esteem.

As she walks into the room, Sharon notices the large basketball backboard attached to the foot of my bed. "Wow, that thing is huge!" she exclaims.

"That's because it came from Texas," I reply with a grin. She rolls her eyes, letting me know my joke fell flat.

"It's awesome that you're sitting up in bed," she says.

"Fifteen more degrees and I'll be ready to transfer from the bed to a wheelchair!" I say enthusiastically.

Setting a bag of presents on the bed, she says, "Merry Christmas" and pulls out a perfectly wrapped gift.

CHAPTER 8

"It *is* a Merry Christmas," I say, bending my left arm to model my gold bracelet.

"You got the bracelet you asked for!"

"I did. What do you think?"

"It's pretty," she says. "Have you decided what date is going on the right side of the bracelet?"

"I'm not sure," I tell her. "Maybe my last day in rehab or the day I—God willing—take my first step."

She smiles, and her excitement shifts from the bracelet to the Christmas gift she brought me. I peel off the wrapping paper to reveal a New International Version (NIV) study Bible.

"It's perfect," I say. "I don't have a study Bible. Thank you so much!"

For the next few minutes, Sharon shows me how to use my new Bible, and I watch her face as she flips back and forth through the pages. Her love of Christ is on full display as she explains how I can use the Bible to study the deeper meaning behind the verses.

When she finishes her tutorial, she places the Bible on the table beside my bed, and I direct her attention to a gift sitting on top of the dresser. I get a kick out of the excitement on her face when she realizes it's a gift for her. She carefully unwraps the box, pulls out the black-and-gray sweater, and holds it against her chest.

"I love it!" she gushes as she leans down to kiss me.

Once I explain how I picked it out, she loves the gift even more. Then she sits down on the side of the bed and grabs my hand. A look of concern replaces her smile.

"I'm transferring to ECU," she announces.

"What? Why?" I ask in disbelief.

"For several reasons, but one is to be closer to you," she replies, waiting for my reaction. Since East Carolina University is in Greenville, her transfer will allow her to be closer to the rehab facility.

"I think that's great!" I say with a grin. "I definitely want to be closer to the girl I'm falling in love with."

She puts both of her hands on my vest and lowers herself down until we're face-to-face. "I'm in love with you too," she whispers. Then we kiss with the passion of two young lovers.

We spend the rest of the day enjoying each other's company. Around five thirty, someone from food services drops off my dinner tray: Salisbury steak, mashed potatoes, and green beans. Sharon cuts up my steak and helps me stab green beans with my fork. Since I was right-handed before my accident, trying to eat with my left hand poses a challenge. To help, the occupational therapy department has provided me with a utensil cuff. The cuff is a Velcro strap that wraps around your hand and holds a utensil in place.

A little after eight o'clock, it's time for Sharon to leave and make the drive back to Vanceboro. For the second time, she tells me she loves me and lets me know that she'll see me soon. Once she leaves, I spend the rest of the evening reminiscing about my day. I decide that, despite being in a rehab center on Christmas, it's been a great day.

CHAPTER 8

○ ○ ○

At seven thirty the next morning, I hear southern belle Althea going in and out of rooms dispensing medications. I've been awake and sitting almost upright since six o'clock because I don't want to experience any issues with my blood pressure when I'm transferred to a wheelchair later this morning. Before leaving for Vanceboro last night, I had Sharon place my running tights and a T-shirt on the railing of my bed even though I'm positive that Althea's going to blow a gasket when she finds out I want to dress in my workout clothes yet again.

Shortly after breakfast, Althea walks into my room, places a few pills on my tongue and a cup of water to my mouth. Standing by the bed while I take my meds, she notices my workout clothes and shakes her head in disbelief, no doubt thinking, *The audacity of this guy.* After she leaves the room, I hear her in the hallway telling another nurse how pointless it is for me to wear workout clothes in bed, especially shoes. I refuse to allow her comments to bother me, but I *am* troubled by how long it's taking the physical therapy department to bring a wheelchair to my room.

Several minutes pass before Althea returns with another nurse, and the two of them get me dressed. It's no simple task to put running tights on my legs, which are deadweight. Luckily, the smoothness of the compression stockings and running tights makes it more manageable. After I'm dressed, I continue to wait for a wheelchair. I try to remain patient and remind myself that it's the day after Christmas and most departments are short-staffed.

Around nine o'clock, an aide from physical therapy shows up with a reclining wheelchair. I want to ask the guy what took so long, but he answers my question before I can ask it, telling me the physical therapy department only has one reclining wheelchair and he couldn't locate it. When I notice that his arms are the size of my legs, I'm glad I didn't ask what took him so long.

"I'm going to go get some help," he says. "Then I'll be back."

"Take your time. I'm in no hurry," I lie. A few minutes later, the aide returns with Kim in tow. "I didn't expect to see you until Friday," I tell her.

"I knew you couldn't wait another day to see me," she replies with a chuckle.

"A physical therapist and a mind reader—clearly, I'm in excellent hands," I say jokingly.

Before the two of them try to transfer me to the wheelchair, Kim hits my call button to ask if an available nurse can come to my room. A few minutes later, my archnemesis shows up. While Althea wraps a blood pressure cuff around my arm, the aide moves the wheelchair next to my bed, then he turns me on my side. As Kim grabs my legs, the two of them spin me around until my lower legs and feet are dangling off the bed. The aide holds me in place while Althea takes my blood pressure. The room spins as I feel the blood leaving my face faster than a flushing toilet.

When I open my eyes, Althea is leaning over me, fanning my face with a medical chart. Lying flat in the bed, I ask, "What happened?"

"You passed out," she says.

CHAPTER 8

"How long have I been out?"

"Not long, just a few seconds."

Kim props up my feet with two pillows and my blood pressure slowly rises, allowing my light-headedness to subside. The three of them agree that the best way to get me in the wheelchair is to move me while keeping my body at a forty-five-degree angle. A few minutes later, Kim and the aide slide me to the edge of the bed. The aide grabs me underneath my arms while Kim puts her hands around my lower legs. Together they ease me from the bed and into the reclining wheelchair, which is reclined at forty-five degrees. When Althea checks my blood pressure, it's low but stable. The aide raises the back of the wheelchair a few degrees then stops to let Althea take my blood pressure again. The process of slowly raising the incline of my wheelchair and taking my blood pressure comes to a halt whenever I try to surpass a forty-five-degree angle. At that point, my blood pressure bottoms out, and a few moments later, I wake up with my face drenched in sweat.

After ten minutes of enduring these blood pressure woes, Althea and Kim put me back in bed. It's clear that I won't be going to physical therapy today. Kim leaves Althea with instructions to continue inclining the bed and keep her informed of my progress. For the next couple hours, the nursing staff tries raising my bed past forty-five degrees but with no success. I get light-headed every time I come close to sitting upright. After two hours of feeling faint, my head is throbbing and I'm exhausted.

My first attempt to get out of bed has been a complete disaster. Kim tries to comfort me, telling me that what I'm experiencing is normal, but I'm not appeased.

In my mind, I see Althea at the nurses station having a spiteful laugh at my failure. *Who am I to argue with her?* I berate myself. *Here I am dressed to go for a run, and I can't even get out of bed.*

The next morning Althea arrives to get me dressed and ready for the day. As she stands by my bed while I take my meds, I notice her looking around the room.

"Where are your workout clothes?" she asks with a smirk.

"No need to rub it in, Althea," I reply glumly.

Althea walks over to my dresser, opens a drawer, and finds my tights and long sleeve T-shirt. "You're gonna have better luck in this outfit today than you did yesterday," she says with a slight smile.

Smiling back at her, I ask, "Does this mean we're friends?"

"Absolutely not," she retorts, shaking her head. She presses the call button and says, "I need some help in 116 to get Mr. Bowen dressed, please."

Once I'm dressed, Althea tries to sit me upright in bed, but the results are the same. I get light-headed, break into a cold sweat, and my blood pressure takes a nosedive. By midmorning, I'm frustrated and discouraged, but I try to remind myself that I've been lying flat for over a month, so it's going to take more than a few hours to get my blood pressure to stabilize while sitting up.

It's late in the morning when Althea slowly sits me upright in bed. I expect a dizzy spell, but this time, there isn't one, nor is there a cold sweat. My blood pressure drops a little, but then it holds steady. Ten minutes pass, and I'm still symptom-free. It's a minor victory, but I'll take it.

CHAPTER 8

Althea calls down to physical therapy and requests the reclining wheelchair and an aide to help transfer me from my bed to the chair. Thirty minutes later, the herculean aide who helped out yesterday arrives, and he and Althea transfer me into the reclining wheelchair. As I quickly sit at a forty-five-degree angle, Althea takes my blood pressure. It's stable, so the aide fastens a large seat belt across my torso to secure me in the wheelchair, then he raises the back of the chair to a ninety-degree angle. When I show no ill effects, the aide tells Althea to call him if she needs further help.

No sooner does he leave the room when the top-heaviness of the halo propels me forward. Reflexively, I reach out with my left arm to catch myself, but the strap holds me safely in place. Unexpectedly, I discover that when I reached out with my left arm, I could feel my right arm move slightly and my abdominal muscles engage.

"Did you see that?" I exclaim, looking at Althea.

"See what?" she asks, confused.

"My right arm . . . it just moved when I reached out to catch myself," I say with disbelief.

"I thought you could already move your right arm," she says.

"No, this is the first time! I also felt my abdominal muscles flex!" I exclaim joyfully. "Althea, you're my lucky charm! And for that, I'm giving you a handful of my get-well pills, aka peanut M&M's."

Althea and I celebrate with a few pieces of candy before she leaves the room to check on her other patients. As she leaves, she tells me I can only stay in the wheelchair for fifteen to twenty minutes at a time. After that, I need to get back in bed to protect the skin on my rear end.

I spend those twenty minutes looking around the room with a new perspective. Who would think to give thanks to God for sitting up straight? But that's exactly what I do.

The twenty minutes go by quickly. Althea returns with Kim, and they transfer me from the wheelchair to my bed. Lying there, I share my big news with Kim and ever so slightly move my right arm and flex my abs. As much as I want to be proud of myself, I know a higher power is at work, so this accomplishment is not mine alone.

Sitting up in bed, I make a mess of my lunch, getting more food *on* me than *in* me. While I eat, I hear the constant hum of voices as some nurses brag about their kids while others talk about what they did for the holidays. I know firsthand the invaluable service nurses provide, but on this morning, an unfamiliar voice is belittling patients. "In 116, there's a weirdo who wears spandex and shoes to bed!" Listening to her snicker, a part of me wants to call her into my room and admonish her, but I realize that would make me no better than she is. Instead, I take the high road. For me, it's imperative that I re-create every aspect of my dream. I saw myself working out with these clothes on, and I *will* wear them every day whether I'm in the bed or out, regardless of what anyone says.

Recently, when my parents arrive for visiting hours, my dad has gotten into the habit of coming to my bedside and asking, "Do you have any good news?"—meaning

CHAPTER 8

has any other part of my body come alive? Today, when he and Mama arrive, Daddy walks into the room, makes a beeline for my bed, and asks, "Hey, Mackel, got any good news for me?"

"Oh, yeah!" I say with excitement. "Put one hand on my belly and the other on my right arm," I instruct. Then I move my right arm and contract my abs for him.

"We've come a long way, baby!" he says with pride.

Not long after my parents arrive, Sharon rushes into the room holding a small plastic bag of craft paints and brushes. She has concocted an idea of painting the rods to my halo like Pixy Stix, the tubes filled with sugary powder that somehow passes for candy. I tell her no way and shake my head. Even if I agreed to let her paint the rods, Dr. A would absolutely refuse. Dejected, she leaves the room, and I realize I've hurt her feelings. I feel bad because I know she's just trying to bring some levity to this difficult time in my life. After several minutes, Sharon returns with a smug look on her face.

"Look Sharon, I know you mean well, but Dr. A will *not* let you paint part of my halo!" I declare.

Laughing, she says, "I checked with the head nurse on duty, and she called Dr. Alsentzer. He said there's no reason I can't paint your rods like Pixy Stix."

"You did not!" I respond in disbelief. "What was the nurse's name?"

"I didn't ask, but I think her name tag said Debbie or Debra. She said she would much rather look at rods painted like Pixy Stix than those tights you wear in bed!" Sharon says with a satisfied smirk.

"Now I know you're lying! She did *not* say that," I respond with a chuckle.

"No, she didn't," Sharon confesses. "But she did contact Dr. Alsentzer, and he gave the okay."

○ ○ ○

Sharon and I spend the next few days together, and I'm grateful for the company. In the days after Christmas, the rehab center is like a ghost town. On Saturday morning, I finally acquiesce and let Sharon paint the rods of my halo to resemble Pixy Stix. Around noon, while Sharon and I are eating lunch, Debra, the head nurse on duty, pops her head in the doorway to ask if I need anything. She immediately notices my striped rods and looks at Sharon, nodding her head to signify a job well done. It's hard to be mad at the nurse who helped save your life!

"Debra, I do need something from you," I respond.

"What do you need?"

"I need a makeup call," I reply.

"A what?"

"It's when a referee, or in your case a nurse, makes a poor judgment call—like giving a patient's girlfriend permission to paint the rods of her boyfriend's halo to look like Pixy Stix. In such a case, a makeup call is required to settle the score," I explain.

Debra finds the humor in my statement and asks what she can do to make it up to me. I ask her for permission to be transferred to my wheelchair long enough to take a stroll around the rehab center with Sharon. Debra smiles and gives the okay.

CHAPTER 8

But as soon as Sharon pushes me across the threshold of my room, I immediately experience a bout of motion sickness. With her help, I lean forward and get some additional blood flow to my head, and soon the dizziness subsides.

A few minutes later, we are slowly meandering down the hallway. I glance inside as we pass by the rooms of other patients. It seems that in every other room, an elderly man or woman is sitting in a wheelchair completely withdrawn from life when they should be active and enjoying their golden years of retirement. But that's what a stroke can rob you of: quality of life.

I close my eyes and say a silent prayer: *God may your spirit work inside these elderly people. Give them the strength to fight and improve their physical and emotional circumstances and the peace to live with the results.* I pray that same prayer for myself. Although I feel God's spirit dwelling inside me, I have a perpetual fear that my faith is not strong enough to allow him to fully pervade my soul, and until I do, I will never reach God's true potential for me or be at peace with whom I'm becoming.

Late on Sunday afternoon, to my surprise, my parents, brother, and grandmother walk into my room and catch Sharon and I in a competitive game of cards. Nervously, I introduce Sharon to my grandmother. I know Gramma's expectations for the girls her grandsons date are almost impossibly high. However, as I watch the two of them interact, Gramma experiences Sharon's genuine personality and takes an instant liking to her.

Turning to Gramma, Daddy says, "Your grandson has something to show you."

Gramma walks over to me, hangs her cane on the side of my bed, and grabs the rail with both hands.

"Gramma, I want you to look at my left arm," I instruct. Then I lift my left arm and place my hand on top of hers.

As Gramma stares at our hands together, I see her eyes well up with tears.

"How 'bout that, Mama? Isn't that good news?" Daddy asks.

"I've been praying every night for this," Gramma says gratefully. "God is good."

"Yes, he is," I reply. "And it won't be long before I'm able to sign my name to that check you gave me."

As we make our way to the cafeteria for dinner, I realize that I'm about to enter a large room filled with people who will undoubtedly stare at the halo attached to my skull, and I feel what I can only describe as a panic attack. My heart races and I become short of breath. When we arrive at the cafeteria, I cautiously peek inside and am relieved to see that the place is nearly empty. It's just after four o'clock, so the lunch bunch has come and gone and the dinner crowd hasn't arrived. As my anxiety abates, I settle down and enjoy dinner with my family. However, this experience leaves me with a newfound respect for those who suffer from anxiety attacks.

Shortly after dinner, my parents, Gramma, and Lee head home, but Sharon sticks around. She's brought Monopoly for our nightly entertainment. Well into our game, Sharon has cornered the housing market, and I'm a few hundred bucks shy of being bankrupt. Fortunately for me, Mike Hamer shows up with one of his

CHAPTER 8

bandmates and his newest acquisition, a hammered dulcimer. With Mike playing the dulcimer and his friend strumming a guitar, Sharon and I enjoy a private concert.

As visiting hours come to an end, Sharon heads back to Vanceboro. By nine o'clock, Mike and I are settled in for the night. Neither one of us has on our TV sets, so the room is quiet. As I try to envision my first day of physical therapy tomorrow, I wonder: *Will I see a physical therapy room that resembles my dream? Or did the viewfinder give me false hope for my future?*

THE VIEWFINDER

CHAPTER 9

MONDAY MORNING ARRIVES, and I'm up early. I lie in bed eagerly awaiting Althea, with my outfit placed at the foot of my bed. I scarf down breakfast expecting her to arrive at any moment, but a few minutes turn into a half hour. Just before I push my call button to find out what the holdup is, Althea and a new morning nurse, Vivian, arrive to give me a sponge bath. I ask Althea if I can skip the "birdbath" because I'm ready for physical therapy, but she refuses, telling me it won't take long. Althea takes off my hospital gown while Vivian notices my Pixy Stix–inspired rods and compliments Sharon's creativity. Althea looks at the painted rods and says with a chuckle, "They're gonna get a kick outta you down in PT."

But it's Althea who gets a kick out of me—literally. Since being fitted with my vest, I have experienced chronic pain in my right shoulder, especially when I'm turned on that side. I haven't complained and for good reason. I've heard nurses whispering in the hallway outside my room regarding patients who grumble too much. Apparently, the nurses don't like whiners.

CHAPTER 9

To give me a bath, Althea and Vivian turn me on one side and push a water-resistant pad underneath me. Then they roll me on the other side and pull it through. I politely ask, "Can you not turn me on my right side? It hurts my shoulder."

"Sweetheart, we gotta turn you on both sides to get the pad underneath you," Althea says in a snippy tone.

I'm naked and lying flat on my back while Vivian stands on the right side of the bed and bends my knees with my feet flat on the bed. Then she reaches over and rotates me toward her while Althea slides the pad underneath me. As they do this, my vest immediately digs deep into my sore shoulder. Without warning, the pain causes both my legs to spasm. My left leg extends behind me, and, like an angry donkey, I kick Althea squarely in the chest! Shocked, I listen as a gasp of air leaves her lungs followed by a series of clumsy footsteps.

As she rushes over to Althea, who is on her way out of the room, Vivian shouts, "Oh my God! Althea, are you alright?"

Immediately, I can hear the loud chatter of nurses as they console Althea in the hallway. I'm lying on my side completely naked, still trying to figure out exactly what just happened. The commotion outside my room has moved down the hall, but my shoulder is throbbing. Luckily, the call button is within reach, so I call for help. "Excuse me, can someone please come roll me off my side? My vest is cutting into my shoulder blade." No response.

Again, I push the call button. "I have a stabbing pain in my shoulder and need help. Please!" There's nothing but radio silence. A couple minutes later, an unfamiliar nurse rushes to my bedside. "Thank God, what took you—"

The nurse leans down to face me at eye level, and before I can utter another word, she snarls, "Do you know who else has a stabbing pain?" When I don't immediately respond, she continues, "Althea, that's who, and it's thanks to you! You're in big trouble, buster."

"I didn't mean—"

"Save it!" she shouts as she turns her back and walks away.

"Can you at least turn me onto my back?" I yelp.

"No! Not right now!" she hollers from the hallway.

I'm still lying naked on my side with my back to the doorway when a second nurse walks into the room. I can't see her, but I sense her standing behind me in silence. I wait as five then ten seconds pass by. Finally, I plead, "Hello! Can you *please* turn me over onto my back?"

A few seconds pass before a nurse says, "Maybe you should've thought about that before you kicked Althea!"

"Thought about *what*?" I respond.

"You do *not* kick nurses!" the nurse scolds, her voice full of anger.

"I didn't mean to. . . . I had a muscle—"

Cutting me off, the nurse says, "Save it!"

"But I didn't—" I shout in frustration.

"You owe Althea a big apology!"

"I *didn't* mean to kick her!" I insist.

CHAPTER 9

As I lie in my bed wearing nothing but my birthday suit, one word comes to mind: *blackballed*. Clearly, the nurses have found me guilty of assault on Althea. *Not a single nurse in the rehab center is going to dress me in my workout clothes after this*, I conclude. *And without wearing those clothes, my vision won't become reality.*

I'm in full pity party mode when, low and behold, Vivian and Althea return to my room. Without a word, Althea rolls me toward her while Vivian grabs the folded half of the pad and pulls it through. Vivian then bathes me while Althea follows behind with a towel drying me off. It's so quiet you can hear a pin drop. After my bath, Althea grabs my compression stockings, and the two of them work together to put them on my legs.

"Althea, I'm sorry I kicked you," I say. "But I didn't do it on purpose; it was a muscle spasm, I swear."

"Well, it looked to me like you got mad 'cause you didn't want to be on your side, so you intentionally kicked me," she responds.

"I would *never* intentionally harm my good luck charm. Can I offer you a few pain pills for your aching chest?" I suggest, pointing to my jar of M&M's.

With that, she smiles and breaks the tension in the room. Althea and Vivian finish getting me dressed, then I wait in bed for someone from the physical therapy department to come get me.

Around a quarter to eight, Kim and an aide show up. As the two of them pick me up and place me in the wheelchair with ease, I wonder how much muscle mass I've lost in the last six weeks. Kim carefully places my feet on the footrests of the chair, and away we go. I'm as nervous as a schoolboy on his first day of kindergarten when I tentatively ask, "Are we going directly to physical therapy?"

"No," Kim replies as she makes a right turn out of my room. "I'm going to give you the grand tour of the rehab facility first."

As we make our way down the hall, the large wooden handrails that line the walls immediately catch my eye. "My first time down this hallway, I saw a girl about my age restrained in a wheelchair and crying to get free."

"That's April," Kim says.

"What's wrong with her?" I ask.

"She has a traumatic brain injury," Kim replies.

"How'd that happen?" I inquire.

"A car accident, I believe."

I learn that April has been here for about six months. Kim tells me it's not uncommon for patients with traumatic brain injuries to spend many months, if not years, in therapy. I think, *How long will I be here? Will I make the most of my time while I'm here?*

When we reach the end of the hallway, the nurses station is on my right. Behind the counter, I catch two nurses looking at me and mumbling to each other. Without a doubt, they're gossiping about my workout clothes and the Pixy Stix rods. I want to kick myself for allowing Sharon to paint my rods. The only thing my wardrobe is missing is a red nose to make me look like a total clown.

As we continue making our way down the hallway, I tell Kim that I was just

CHAPTER 9

down this hall yesterday, people-watching with my girlfriend. Kim confirms what Sharon and I suspected: this wing is for stroke patients. The end of the hallway opens up to a multipurpose room, where Kim informs me that recreational therapy and other activities take place.

We make a U-turn and head toward the front entrance of the rehab center. On the other side of the lobby entrance, I see the offices of Dr. Alsentzer, his PAs, and other administrative staff. Kim points out the office of Dr. Duncan, the rehab center's psychologist, and tells me that I'll be working with him two times a week for biofeedback therapy, whatever that is.

As we continue our tour, we turn left down the main hallway that connects the rehab center to the hospital. The office of Jim Barrett, the recreational rehab therapist, is on the left. Up ahead, I see the sign for physical and occupational therapy. The closer we get to the door, the faster my heart beats. If the inside of the room looks nothing like my dream, it'll be a huge letdown.

At the entrance, Kim reaches over and pushes a button, and I watch as the double doors automatically open. As I quickly scan the room, I'm astonished by the similarities between what the physical therapy room actually looks like and the image from my dream a few weeks earlier. The low, padded tables and the chrome parallel bars placed in front of a large mirror are just as I imagined. In awe, I think to myself, *If this is a sign from God of things to come, I can't wait to live out the rest of my dream.*

Kim wheels me alongside a wall, parks my wheelchair, and informs me that the first of two sessions of physical therapy is just getting started. Scoping out the room, I notice a few patients staring at me, no doubt scrutinizing my attire. Several of them are still wearing hospital gowns while others dress in street clothes. From the pity expressed on many of their faces, I can tell they believe my eagerness to work out will soon turn to disappointment.

As I wait for my PT session to begin, I realize that I'm at a crossroads in my life—not unlike the pivotal moment when I quit my job at the sawmill—and I can travel down one of two paths with my physical therapy: On the road most traveled, I can put forth a minimal amount of effort and rationalize why I can't be successful. Or I can take the road less traveled, which means every day I do my very best without quitting and without regret while acknowledging the possibility that I might still fail. For me, the choice is simple because God has already made that choice for me. I'm no longer suffering from complete paralysis nor am I in excruciating pain. I believe God has a plan for my life; I just don't know what it is yet.

To me, the road less traveled means I won't let the negative vibes of other patients or staff members—or anyone—deter me from working hard every chance I get. Although some may see me as a quadriplegic and unable to walk, I see myself as a partially able-bodied man who has the potential to one day walk again. When the going gets tough, I will remind myself that it takes the same amount of energy to dwell on negative thoughts as it does on positive ones, but the consequences of the two are entirely different. This reminds me of the motto I came up with: "Take one day at a time. All day long, do your very best, and let God worry about the rest." If it's God's will that I never get out of this wheelchair, so be it. But a poor attitude, a

CHAPTER 9

refusal to give my very best, and lack of self-discipline will not take root in my mind.

The physical therapy room is full of patients, many of whom are elderly and have suffered strokes. Some have partial paralysis and can walk, but others are confined to wheelchairs because their injuries are too severe. One woman stands out to me. She's sitting lethargically in a wheelchair near the wall. Her ash-colored hair is matted to her head, and a stroke has caused the left side of her face to droop. Two frail legs poke out from beneath her polyester slacks. Her legs are so thin that they can't hold up her knee-high stockings, so they dangle around her ankles. Her condition is heartbreaking to me. I want to walk over and tell her that everything is going to be okay, but who am I kidding? I can't walk and to tell her things will work out fine would be a lie.

Scattered around the room, I count half a dozen patients with spinal cord injuries. From the looks of it, most of them are paraplegics, meaning they have paralysis from the waist down. Although we are unique individuals, we share one common trait: we're all paralyzed. While it's not the club I want to be a part of, I must accept that I am. The one bright spot I see in the room is Mike Hamer. When we make eye contact, he gives me a nod and smiles as if we just ran into each other at the local gym.

When the first session ends and the group of patients disperses, Kim wheels me over to a padded table, then she and an aide transfer me. I lie flat on my back while she does a complete physical evaluation. Afterward, she praises the progress I've made since she started working with me over at the hospital. With humility, I tell her I wish I could take credit for the improvements, but it has come from a higher power.

Next she works my spastic muscles through a series of range-of-motion exercises. Moving my limbs back and forth reduces the spasticity, which decreases my pain, but also fatigues my muscles.

"Why do my muscles fatigue so easily?" I question.

"Atrophy produces weak muscles, and weak muscles tire easily," Kim explains.

"How much do you think I weigh?" I ask out of curiosity.

"My guess is between 130 and 140," she replies. "How much did you weigh before your accident?"

I sigh deeply and reply, "A lot more—160 pounds."

"We're going to have to fatten you up then!" she says with a laugh.

My one-hour physical therapy session flies by. Once I'm back in my chair, Kim wheels me over to the adjoining occupational therapy room and introduces me to Brandy, my occupational therapist. Like Kim, she begins a patient-centered assessment that helps her create a profile of my functional deficits and desired goals. The tests reveal that my left hand and wrist show a fair amount of strength. However, I'm very clumsy when Brandy puts me through a series of dexterity tests. The lack of sensation in my left hand is a significant roadblock. I can slightly move my right wrist, but I still have paralysis in the fingers of that hand.

After our session, Brandy wheels me back to my room. While waiting for my lunch to arrive, I think about the woman I observed in the physical therapy room this morning, and I'm flooded with feelings of empathy toward her. It's the third time since I've been here that I've experienced this overwhelming feeling of

CHAPTER 9

compassion for someone. I felt it within minutes of arriving at the rehab center when I saw the elderly man slouched over with his head against the railing, and then again, only moments later, I felt it when I passed by April pulling at her restraints.

I realize that I'm changing, but I wonder if my softened heart is solely a by-product of what I've endured over the past six weeks or if it's part of God's plan to mold my personality so I can fulfill his purpose for me. I don't know the answer to this question, but what I *do* know is that a conversion from selfishness to selflessness is taking place in my heart and mind.

Not long after I finish lunch, there's a knock on my door and a man pokes his head into the room and says, "Hey, Mr. Bowen. My name is Dr. Duncan, and I'm a psychologist here at the rehab center. How are you today?"

"Pretty good," I reply.

"Great. We're going to take a stroll down to my office. Can you wheel yourself, or do you need help?"

"I'm going to need some help," I respond.

"No problem, glad to do it."

On the way to Dr. Duncan's office, he asks me how I got injured. I tell him a car accident. Hearing me describe the outfit I was wearing when the paramedics arrived produces a huge laugh. But once we're in his office, his questions change from casual to probing. He asks me about my relationship with my mother, father, brother, and girlfriend. When he asks if there have been changes in my relationships with my family since the accident, I tell him yes, especially with my dad. I explain that before my accident, I rarely thought about my mom or dad until I needed something. In college, I called them every Sunday night and spoke to them for a few minutes. They wanted to make sure I was okay, and I wanted to ask for money. But since my accident, I realize the enormous sacrifices my parents have made and the unconditional love they have for my brother and me.

"You mentioned a big change in the relationship between you and your dad. How so?" Dr. Duncan asks.

"Before my accident, I wasn't sure if my father loved me," I begin. "I was a hellion growing up and was always getting into trouble. But our relationship started to change the day of my accident. My first night at the rehab center, I became deathly sick and prayed to die. I told my parents I was giving up. I also told them I loved them. I hadn't said those three words to my dad since I was a small boy. My father told me how much he loved me and said we would make it through this together. Happily, knock on wood, we have by taking things one day at a time."

"Why do you say you were a hellion growing up?" Dr. Duncan asks.

I grin and say, "We don't possibly have enough therapy sessions for me to explain."

He smiles back at me then switches gears and asks another question. "Has there been a change in your relationship with your mother since the accident?"

"Yes, but not in terms of whether or not I think she loves me," I respond. "Unlike my dad, I've always been able to tell my mom that I love her. Our relationship has changed recently because I now recognize how selfless my mother has been for so many years."

CHAPTER 9

I tell Dr. Duncan that while in the hospital in Wilmington, I noticed my mom wearing one of my old sweater vests with a blouse she's had for at least a decade. Rambling on about my mother, I explain how she spent most of her time cleaning and cooking meals for us seven days a week. Dr. Duncan is skeptical when I tell him that, growing up, my brother and I never experienced a family meal at a sit-down restaurant. The closest we came was sitting in the family car, eating hamburgers my dad had picked up at the Hardee's drive-through on the way to visit my aunt and uncle.

"Speaking of your brother, how's your relationship with him?" Dr. Duncan probes.

"Lee's always had my back, and I'm proud to call him my brother. He's also very talented," I say with obvious admiration.

"In what way?"

I tell him that Mama and Daddy couldn't afford to buy us toys, so my brother would make our toys. To drive my point home, I recall the time Lee made an electric go-cart from the motor off my dad's table saw. Dr. Duncan laughs in disbelief.

We talk briefly about my relationship with Sharon, and then the question I've been waiting for rolls off his lips, "So, I understand you played college tennis before your accident. At what age did you pick up a racket?"

"I'd rather not talk about tennis if that's okay," I reply.

"I understand," he says. Then he shifts the conversation in yet another direction by asking, "You said earlier that you became sick when you got here and prayed to die. If you'd had the opportunity, do you think you would've taken your own life?"

"Yes," I admit.

"Are you a spiritual person?"

"I am now," I say.

"Interesting," he says, pondering my response. At that point, the probing questions stop, and Dr. Duncan rolls a small machine toward me. "Michael, have you ever heard of biofeedback?"

"No. What is it?" I ask.

He explains that biofeedback is a technique which teaches patients how to control certain bodily functions, such as heart rate, breathing, and skin temperature. Learning to control these processes can help reduce stress and manage chronic pain. When Dr. Duncan asks me if I'd be interested in learning this technique, I tell him yes, so he places several electrodes on my skin and a pulse sensor on my finger. He tells me I'll hear a series of tones, and my goal is to slow down these tones by taking slow, deep breaths and relaxing.

I close my eyes and take myself to a tranquil place. For me, it's sitting in my favorite lounge chair on Wrightsville Beach watching the sunset. In my serene place, the summer heat has diminished and soft rays of light reflect off the calm ocean water like fireflies. Groups of brown pelicans fly by in unison, hovering just inches over the rolling surf. The beach has emptied of tourists, and all I can hear is the hypnotizing sound of the waves rolling onto the shore.

Within a couple of minutes, the sounds of the tones coming out of the

CHAPTER 9

biofeedback machine grow further apart, which means my heart rate is dropping. My ability to lower my heart rate impresses Dr. Duncan. I tell him it's much easier to imagine that I'm relaxing at the beach than it is to sit here with him. Appreciating my dry sense of humor, he laughs.

My therapy session ends with instructions from Dr. Duncan to continue working on my breathing technique at night before bedtime. When we leave his office, he rolls me down the hallway to see Jim Barrett, the head recreational therapist.

Mr. Barrett smiles and says hello, and I instantly notice the sparkle in his brown eyes. I introduce myself and extend my left hand. He quickly draws his left hand from his pocket and shakes mine.

Dr. Duncan leaves, and Mr. Barrett fills me in on the variety of activities that take place during recreational therapy. Although he is soft-spoken, he talks passionately about the program. I can see he's an optimist, so I'm immediately attracted to his personality.

"You're a tennis player, right?" he asks.

"I was before my accident," I say dejectedly.

"Great! On Thursday nights, there's a round-robin Ping-Pong tournament in the psychiatric ward. Maybe you could join us?" he asks excitedly.

"Why are the Ping-Pong tables in the psychiatric ward?"

Jim, as he requests I call him, laughs heartily and responds, "Are you kidding? There are half a dozen psych patients who love playing Ping-Pong. It's great therapy."

Jim wheels me down to the multipurpose room where arts and crafts, bingo, and board games take place as part of therapy. He also informs me that there are outings to the local bowling alley for adaptive bowling and aquatics at the YWCA. On Friday nights, patients go out to eat at a different themed restaurant. At the moment, the thought of going outside the walls of the rehab center scares me. I look like I belong in a freak show.

My therapy session wraps up at four, so Jim wheels me back to my room. As my first day of rehab comes to an end, I settle into my room, TV remote in hand, and channel surf for an hour until I notice a figure standing in the doorway. It's my college roommate, David McGee.

"McGee, what are you doing here?" I ask, totally surprised.

"Hey, Bowen. What's up, brother? I heard there are some good-looking nurses around here, so I thought I'd stop by and check them out before you run them off," he says with a playful grin.

I haven't seen McGee since I left Wilmington, so his visit makes me realize how much I miss my friends and teammates.

"I brought you a belated Christmas gift," he says with a sly smile.

"What kind of gift?" I ask, shocked because the guys on the team don't exchange gifts.

"Well, it's not the new set of front teeth you asked for from Santa," he jokes. Reaching into a plastic bag, he pulls out an animated stuffed dog. He turns it on, and we both laugh as the dog moves its nose while barking out a Christmas tune. Then he reaches back into his bag and takes out a tan-and-navy blue Fila warm-up suit.

CHAPTER 9

"Merry Christmas. Now you have your own," he says, subtly implying that he's tired of me borrowing his Fila suit.

When McGee asks how I'm doing, I share some details of what has transpired since I left New Hanover Regional Medical Center. He shakes his head in disbelief of the setbacks I've endured. We lighten up the conversation and chat about a few guys on the team and their mischievous behavior. He tells me that some people around campus have asked how I'm doing—even a couple of girls.

When I inform McGee that Sharon has transferred from UNC–Wilmington to ECU to be closer to her family and me, he replies, "That's not good."

"Why not?" I ask.

"Because I told an old girlfriend of yours yesterday that it would be okay for her to stop by and visit you tonight," he says casually.

"You better be joking!" I exclaim.

"I'm not. She said she'd stop by around seven."

"McGee, you better be lying!"

"Brother, you need to comb your hair and take those ridiculous looking bolts out of your head before she gets here," he says with a grin. His comic jab sends me into a laughing spell that takes my breath away.

Out of all the guys on the team, McGee and I go back the furthest. We met in the fall of 1981 on my first day at Mount Olive Junior College. My parents had just dropped me off, and I was walking through the lobby of the men's dormitory with my suitcase in one hand and my tennis bag in the other. When I glanced to my left, I saw a guy sitting in a recliner against the wall. He was dressed in full military fatigues and sported a haircut that was just shy of leaving him bald. Propped against his chair was a large military-issued duffel bag full of clothes.

As I walked by, I could sense him staring at me. Then I heard GI Joe ask, "Hey, is your last name Bowen?"

I stopped, turned, and put my hands up. "Yes, it is. Don't shoot!"

He chuckled in response and said, "My name's David McGee. I'm your roommate."

"Please tell me you're in the army," I said.

"National Guard," he replied. "I just got back from two weeks of training, and I'm in desperate need of a shower." We both laughed, and that was the beginning of a lifelong friendship. We even transferred to UNC–Wilmington and continued as roommates.

Checking his watch, McGee tells me he needs to take off because he's heading to Rocky Mount to see his folks. As he walks to the door, joking aside, I sincerely thank him for the gifts and the visit. With a serious expression on his face, he looks at me and says, "Find a comb and a wrench. Your ex-girlfriend will be here later tonight."

For the next hour, I shoot hoops, wait for dinner, and ponder whether McGee is crazy enough to send an old girlfriend to visit me tonight. Dinner comes and goes with no ex-girlfriend in sight. By seven thirty, I'm lying in bed searching for something to watch on TV.

But then it dawns on me that I'm not living up to my motto. *How can I do*

CHAPTER 9

my best all day long if I lie in bed after visiting hours are over? What are the chances that Dr. Alsentzer and the nursing staff will let me stay in my wheelchair and exercise after visiting hours are over? I wonder. I realize there's a high probability that the answer will be no, especially since I still have one foot in the doghouse because of my earlier "assault" on Althea.

But the way I see it, I have enough strength in my left leg, hand, and arm to move my wheelchair forward and backward one foot at a time. Since the rehab hallways are empty at night, why couldn't I use the handrails in the halls to push and pull my wheelchair around the rehab center?

I hit the call button and ask to see Debra. When she comes in, I make my case to her about the physical benefits of staying in my wheelchair at night and working out. She's receptive but tells me Dr. Alsentzer will need to approve it. I figure it'll take days to get an answer from him, but Lady Luck shines upon me. Debra phones Dr. A, and he gives the okay for me to stay in my chair at night for an hour but with a caveat: He insists that a nurse boost me up every fifteen to twenty minutes while I'm in the wheelchair, and if I get any sores on my butt from sitting in the chair, the deal is off.

Shortly after getting the doctor's approval, two nurses stop by my room, transfer me into my wheelchair, and push me to the hallway so that the railing is on my left side. With my left hand, I pull myself down the hallway, one foot at a time. After traveling twenty-five feet, my left hand is exhausted. I'm twenty-five feet away from my room, but it might as well be twenty-five miles. Since I'm stranded, I sit there and watch the nurses go about their jobs. The staff members are all part of a fine-tuned machine. They methodically work their way up and down the hallway delivering meds, switching out IV bags, and emptying urinals and bedpans. It's a selfless job that requires a unique skill set. While the nurses are busy with these tasks, call button lights outside patient rooms flash like fireflies. After ten minutes of sitting in the hallway, I flag down a nurse who wheels me to my room and helps me get into bed. Within a few minutes, exhaustion sets in and sleep prevails. It's been a great day.

New Year's Eve day is uneventful. I attend my physical and occupational therapy sessions, but a lot of patients don't show up. Kim explains that it's not uncommon for patients to go on family outings during the holidays.

Visiting hours are also extended during the holidays. Sharon shows up around four, and my parents arrive about an hour later. I ask if Lee's coming, but Daddy says he doesn't think so because there's a big New Year's Eve bash downtown at the convention center tonight. Although a part of me is jealous, I'm happy for my brother.

Since it is New Year's Eve, Daddy suggests that the four of us go out to K&W for dinner, but I tell him I'm not ready. I haven't ventured outside the confines of the rehab center for a reason: I don't want people to stare at me. To appease me, we settle on having dinner in the hospital cafeteria. I figure that since it's New Year's Eve, very few people will be eating there.

As expected, the cafeteria is almost empty, so we get our food and enjoy each

CHAPTER 9

other's company. Sharon talks about the academic challenges of school, and my parents tell us they are making plans to go camping at the beach for the entire month of July down at the Salter Path Family Campground. They insist Sharon come and spend a weekend with them. Jokingly, I ask them if I can tag along. Other than that, I just listen, thankful to have family around me.

After dinner, Sharon announces that she has to leave. She's staying with her parents in Vanceboro and has promised to be home before dark. Mama and Daddy planned to stay until midnight and ring in the new year with me, but I convince them that they need to go home too. I'm tired and probably won't stay up until midnight anyway. When they leave around eight, I get set to spend the evening with Dick Clark.

I turn on the TV but drift off to sleep while I wait for *Dick Clark's New Year's Rockin' Eve* special to come on. Shortly before nine o'clock, I'm shaken awake by my brother.

"You can't go to sleep! We have to ring in the new year together!" he insists.

"What are you doing here? Daddy said you were going to a party downtown," I reply.

"No, the party is right here," he says as he pulls two small champagne bottles from his jacket.

Lying on my side with the champagne bottle propped against my vest and a long straw between my lips, my brother and I sip on bubbly together and watch the ball drop on Times Square as 1985 ends and 1986 begins.

THE VIEWFINDER

CHAPTER 10

By the second week of January, I am settled into a routine that includes a variety of therapies during the day and pushing and pulling myself around the rehab center at night. I can tell that I'm getting stronger every day. Daddy is like a proud papa every time I show the smallest amount of progress. Staying faithful to my dream, I wear my gold bracelet and dress in my running tights, a long-sleeved T-shirt, and Nike sneakers every day. I'm sure the patients and staff wonder when these get washed. Although I still occasionally get stares and chuckles because of my attire, I don't let it bother me.

In physical therapy, Kim is having me use a combination of resistance bands, free weights, and machine weights to strengthen the left side of my body. At this point, my left hand and arm are strong enough to lift ten-pound dumbbells several times. I can also hold all my weight on my left leg for a few seconds, but I have little ability to balance myself.

In a seated position, my abdominal muscles are powerful enough that I can bend at the waist, slide my hands to my knees, and sit up straight. Although I have

CHAPTER 10

traces of movement in my right arm and leg, it's not enough for it to be functional. Compounding my limited mobility is my loss of sensation. It makes everything more difficult, and I've found myself acutely aware of the absence of a loving touch. Despite these tribulations, I stay true to my motto and remind myself not to dwell on my challenges and limitations.

A week before, I was tired after one session of physical therapy. Now, with increased muscular strength and improved stamina, I want to push myself even more. Inspired by my progress, I ask Kim if I can start coming to both sessions of physical therapy in the mornings. She agrees but says that during the first session of PT, I'll have to work mostly on my own since she has to work with her scheduled patients. To further fulfill my commitment to work from sunup to sundown, I decide that I'll start wheeling myself to physical therapy in the mornings instead of having someone else do it for me.

The next time I see Althea, I ask my newfound friend if she'll get me up and dressed early enough to attend the first session of physical therapy. When she asks me why I'm switching from the second session to the first, I tell her I'm not; I'll be attending both sessions from now on. Althea gapes at me incredulously then rolls her eyes and looks up at the ceiling. "Why me, Lord?" she mouths. Although she agrees to get me up early, she insists this stunt is going to cost me some M&M's.

On the morning of Monday, January 13, Althea and Nurse Sharon get me dressed, fed, and transferred to my wheelchair by seven thirty. The first session of physical therapy starts at eight. Since the PT room is about a hundred yards—a minute's walk—from my room, I estimate that it'll take me thirty minutes to wheel myself there.

I'm excited about the morning's challenge. With the increased strength in my left quad, I determine that it's better to go down the hall backward so I can push off with my left leg and use my left hand and arm on the handrails. It's slow going, but by the ten-minute mark, I've traveled thirty feet. However, just as my confidence is building, fatigue triggers a spasm in my right ankle. I try to stop the involuntary movement by using my left hand to push down on my right knee, but the spasm is stronger than my fatigued hand and arm. The more I fight to stop the spasm, the more rapidly it pulsates. Eventually, the extreme palpations send my right foot traveling off the footrest of my wheelchair. I lean forward and try to lift my right leg to return my foot to the footrest, but I'm unsuccessful. Even worse, the weight of my halo and vest coupled with my weak abdominal muscles pulls my torso down to my knees. At this point, I'm in a real pickle. Two people pass by before I can ask for help. Thinking the third time's a charm, I stop the next person who walks by.

"Excuse me, can you help me?" I ask a maintenance worker.

"You need some help sitting up?" he inquires.

"I do. If you grab the back of my vest, you should be able to pull me upright," I instruct.

After he pulls me to a sitting position and places my foot back on the footrest, I ask him if he'll push me the short distance to physical therapy. Even though I'm disappointed that I didn't make it to PT on my own, the feeling of being fatigued

CHAPTER 10

exhilarates me. I realize that this morning I bit off more than I could chew, and getting myself to physical therapy will not happen overnight. However, I take consolation knowing that I did wheel myself thirty feet without help.

The next morning, I break down my trek to therapy into steps so it's an attainable goal, then I have Althea wheel me to about fifty feet shy of the PT room. For someone with functional legs, it's a ten-second walk to the doors. Dressed in my running tights, I look like I should just be able to hop up from this wheelchair and jog to therapy. Instead, it takes about every ounce of my strength to slowly roll myself backward, twelve inches at a time, toward my destination.

I have decided that today, failure is not an option. If it takes me all day to travel fifty feet to get through the doors of the PT room, then so be it. Thirty feet into my journey I'm tired, but I'm experiencing no spasms. At forty feet, the wheels to my chair are creeping forward as I take brief breaks between every push and pull. Nine minutes and forty seconds after I began, I reach the entrance to the physical therapy room. I feel more tired than I've ever been in my life, but I did it. It's a minor victory, but it's *my* victory.

Once I'm inside the room, Kim sees me and comes to my rescue. She wheels me over against the wall until she can assist me. While I sit and recover, I mentally compute how long it'll take me to wheel from my room to physical therapy. It took me just under ten minutes to travel fifty feet this morning, so it'll probably take me at least an hour to go the full distance. Instead of discouraging me, this challenge excites me. For the first time since my accident, I have personally set a short-term goal. I go to PT five days a week, so each time I go, I'll increase the distance I wheel myself by twenty feet. At that pace, I should be able to achieve my goal in just over two weeks.

During the first session of physical therapy, Kim has me work with resistance bands. While I'm working out, I notice an old, gray stationary bike that's missing the seat and post. From my vantage point across the room, it looks like I could situate my wheelchair behind the pedals and move them with my feet—assuming I have the strength to keep my feet *on* the pedals.

When Kim walks by, I ask, "What's the deal with the stationary bike in the corner?"

"It's old and needs a seat," she replies.

"Will it pedal?"

She says she thinks it will, so I ask her to push me over to it. As I get a closer look at the bike, an idea hits me: if Kim can find something to strap my left foot to the pedal, maybe I can rotate the cranks of the bike. So she positions me behind the stationary bike, removes both footrests from my wheelchair, and attaches my left foot to the pedal with an Ace bandage.

My first attempt at moving the pedals is unsuccessful. My left leg feels like spaghetti, so I wait a few minutes, hoping my leg will regain some strength. I try again, but the pedal crank arms still won't budge an inch! Inspecting the stationary bike, I notice a resistance knob that when engaged makes it harder to pedal. *I wonder if that's the problem.*

CHAPTER 10

I ask an aide to turn the knob and release any resistance to the front wheel. With my left foot secured to the pedal, I close my eyes and envision myself rotating the bicycle's crank arms. I rock the pedal back and forth, moving the crank arms a couple of inches. After a minute, I rest and start again. As the first session of physical therapy ends, I have increased my rocking motion up to six or seven inches. *Two victories in one day!* I think to myself. To the average Joe, this small feat might seem insignificant. But to me, it's an important stepping stone toward walking again.

By the start of the second hour of physical therapy, I'm too drained to complete any of my lower body exercises, so Kim thoroughly stretches my weary legs and puts them through their range-of-motion exercises.

When Mama and Daddy arrive for visiting hours, I'm eager to share my news with them. But before I can tell them about my breakthroughs in physical therapy, Dr. Alsentzer and his PA Mike Bousman knock on my door.

Dr. A does a quick physical assessment of my physical strength, and they are both pleased with my progress. However, Dr. A tells me he's concerned with the increasing pressure in my bladder. In my medical chart the past few days, both James and Charles have noted having difficulty getting a catheter in and out of my spastic bladder. As a result, Dr. A prescribes a medication to relax my bladder and sphincter muscle so that I can continue to in-and-out cath. "We'll give this new drug a couple days to do its thing," he says in his German accent. "But if it doesn't work, you'll have to go back on a Foley catheter." I ask Dr. A what percentage of patients with spinal cord injuries regain control of their bladder. He tells me around 20 percent. Before leaving, he grabs a Nerf ball off my bed, takes a shot, and tells me to keep working hard in therapy. His shot is a brick. As he walks out the door, I sarcastically tell him to keep working hard on his shot.

The news that Dr. A plans to put in a Foley if the newly prescribed medicines do not reduce the pressure in my spastic bladder threatens to overshadow my good news. What's so frustrating is that I can feel when my bladder is full, I just can't empty it. But Mama and Daddy remind me of my motto, so I do my best to put the negative thoughts out of my head and enjoy our time together. To get my mind off the bad news, I tell them about wheeling myself part of the way to PT and pedaling on the stationary bike.

Before going to sleep tonight, I pray to God for the strength to live up to my motto. I ask him for the willpower to turn over my feelings of worry, fright, and uncertainty to Christ. I pray for peace in whatever the outcome may be. As the clock strikes midnight, James the crafty "cath man" shows up to take care of me. For some reason, I feel compelled to share my bladder woes with him.

"Hey, James. How's it going, man?" I greet.

"It's goin', my brother," he replies while putting on sterile gloves.

"Let me ask you something. Dr. A told me that if the medicine he prescribed doesn't reduce the pressure in my bladder, he's going to put in a Foley catheter." But before I can ask my question, he answers it for me.

"Brother, you don't want no Foley catheter in you for the rest of your days.

CHAPTER 10

Trust me," James says with a facial expression that looks like he bit into something sour. "What you drinkin' during the day?"

"I drink whatever the nurses give me, which is mostly water and some cranberry juice," I respond.

He shakes his head at my answer. "Listen, you need my special concoction."

"What's that?" I ask.

"Mix you up half cranberry juice, half prune juice, and a splash of ginger ale. You drink that *all* day for a couple days, and you'll be peein' like a racehorse," he says with a smile. With that, James finishes catheterizing me and is off to his next patient.

As soon as he leaves the room, I push the call button and ask the nurse, "Can I get a can of cranberry juice, prune juice, and ginger ale?"

"It's after midnight," she replies, dumbfounded by my request.

"I know it's late, but I really need these drinks," I respond with a trace of desperation in my voice.

After a few seconds of silence, she says, "I can bring you a can of cranberry juice and ginger ale, but we don't have any prune juice."

"I'll take it. Thank you so much!"

A few minutes later, the nurse brings me the cranberry juice and ginger ale and mixes them in a large, insulated cup. I chug it down immediately. By early morning, I can tell my bladder is full, but despite pushing on my abdomen, I have no urge to pee.

At six o'clock, James shows up to cath me again before his shift ends. When he asks if I tried his concoction, I tell him the nurse filled a cup with cranberry juice and ginger ale, but she didn't have any prune juice. James picks up the phone in my room and pushes a few buttons.

"Who's this?" he asks, holding the phone receiver to his ear as he waits for a response. "Angie, hey, it's James. Is Big Mike workin' this mornin'?"

After a few moments of silence, James continues, "Big Mike, it's James. What's happenin', brother? I need a favor. Will you find the breakfast tray for a Michael Bowen in rehab room 116 and add a couple cans of prune juice to his order?"

James hangs up the phone and tells me Big Mike is going to hook me up. Before leaving my room, he reminds me to drink the cocktail throughout the day, and I thank him profusely for looking out for me. Just after seven, my breakfast—including the prune juice—arrives. While I eat, Althea blends my juices and ginger ale in a thermos.

After she gets me dressed and transfers me to my wheelchair, Althea drops me off about seventy-five feet away from the entrance to physical therapy. Using my left leg, I push my wheelchair backward and at the same time, use my left hand to push off on the handrail. I reach the door to PT in just over sixteen minutes.

Once inside, I make my way over to the stationary bike, and Kim follows right behind me with an Ace bandage to wrap my left foot to the pedal. Perched in my wheelchair, I use my left foot to rock the crank arms back and forth, gathering more momentum with each push and pull. I get close to turning the crank arms over, but fatigue sets in and I have to stop. While I'm resting, Kim walks over and

CHAPTER 10

tells me not to wear myself out like I did yesterday because she has other work for me to do today. Heeding her advice, I take a break and polish off my thermos of juice and ginger ale.

When the second session of PT starts, Kim wants to know if I'm up for a challenge, and I tell her, "Of course!" However, I'm a little apprehensive when she says she wants me to transfer from my wheelchair to the padded table without her help. The table is a couple inches lower than the seat of my wheelchair, so this feat requires the use of a transfer board, which looks like a miniature surfboard that's about three feet long. To demonstrate how to use it, Kim brings over an empty wheelchair and places it a couple feet to the right of the table. Seated parallel to the table, she flips up the chair's footrests and places her feet flat on the floor. Next, she removes the chair's left armrest, and I watch her intently as she pushes one end of the board underneath her left butt cheek while allowing the other end of the board to rest on the table, creating a bridge between the two. Then she lifts herself out of the chair and scoots across the board onto the table.

With confidence, I look at her and say, "Piece of cake."

Kim rolls her wheelchair away and puts my chair in its place. Then she helps me remove the left armrest. I eagerly grab the board and place it under my left butt cheek while she puts a thick safety belt around my chest and situates herself behind me. On her signal, I use my left leg to lift and scoot both butt cheeks onto the board, but I immediately fall backward into Kim's arms. Not only do I have no abdominal strength, I also have no sense of balance. After placing me upright on the board, Kim helps me finish making my way to the table. Needless to say, it's a humbling experience for me.

Kim's next challenge is for me to stand on my left leg, pivot my foot around, and sit down on the table. Again, Kim shows me how to perform the maneuver, and I marvel at how easy she makes it look. This time, she stands in front of me, gripping the safety belt firmly. Once I stand up, I'm as wobbly as a Weeble. But unlike the famous roly-poly toy from the 1970s, I do fall down. When my left knee buckles, Kim and the aide lower me back into my wheelchair. Disappointed, I sit and stare straight ahead, distraught by what just took place.

"You did great!" Kim says with encouragement. "I hardly had to help you out of the chair!"

The aide adds, "Yeah, you made that look easy."

I look up at them and say, "Neither of you should pursue a life of crime because you're both terrible liars." With desperation in my voice, I ask Kim, "How will I ever learn to walk again when I have no sensation from the neck down and no ability to balance?"

Hearing the frustration in my voice, the two of them do their best to reassure me that this is the beginning of a long process. Even so, I leave physical therapy feeling dejected. Then I spend my time in occupational therapy ruminating on the thought of wearing a Foley catheter and leg bag for the rest of my life, which only adds to my despair.

My despondency continues after lunch as I mope into group therapy guilt-ridden

CHAPTER 10

because I'm the only person there with an incomplete spinal cord injury who can move his legs. Everyone else there with a spinal cord injury will likely use a wheelchair for the rest of their lives, barring some divine intervention. However, as I recall the disastrous results of my therapy session this morning, I reason that chances are I'll never walk again either.

In group therapy, Dr. Duncan asks us to ponder the question: how has your injury impacted your life? Marty, a complete quad who is dependent on a ventilator and can only move his head and neck, speaks first. His goal is to further his education and become a counselor for drug addicts. Robert goes next. He tells the group that before breaking his back by falling off a ladder, he was a self-employed contractor. With brutal honesty, he says, "I don't know what I'm going to do. I have horrible health insurance, and I'm spending my life savings to be here."

Wayne was a veteran paramedic before his injury. Four weeks ago, EMS dispatched him and his partner to a single-car accident. In inclement weather, a car had slid off the road and hit a telephone pole. Wayne didn't see the power line draped across the hood of the vehicle, so when he touched the car, it electrocuted him. The jolt of electricity blew off his right ear, right fingers, and all the toes on his right foot. As a result, he had no choice but to retire.

When it's my turn, I tell the group that before my injury, I was a student at UNC–Wilmington and a member of the tennis team. My plan was to graduate in May with a degree in physical education and find a job teaching as a tennis pro. Now, I explain, those plans are about as dead as the sensation in my body.

Mike Hamer follows me, and of course, his testimony is the bright spot in the group. He tells us he's looking forward to teaching English at ECU once again and resuming his music career with his band.

Despite Mike's optimistic response, the mood in the room is understandably somber. No one tries to find a silver lining somewhere in our misery, not even Dr. Duncan. Thanking us for our candor, he tells us Jim Barrett will lead group therapy next week. As Dr. Duncan pushes me back to my room, he encourages me to continue working on meditative breathing and applying deep massages to my abdomen to stimulate my bladder.

Back in my room, I ask a nurse to mix up another thermos of James's brew. I'm not in the mood to socialize, so I skip recreational therapy. Instead, I sit in my chair and drink my mixture of juices and ginger ale while pushing on my abdomen and practicing my relaxation techniques. Silently, I pray, *Dear Father, you know what I'm feeling right now. Take this self-pity from me. Your blessings have brought me this far. If it's not your will that I gain the use of my bladder and bowels, then so be it. But grant me peace either way.*

I spend the late afternoon fighting off the feelings of hopelessness that I know will hinder my recovery. I find my mind jumping from one irrational thought to another: *What happens when my Foley springs a leak while I'm out to dinner? I wonder if Marty is more concerned about getting a stupid leak in his leg bag or a malfunction in the pump of the ventilator that keeps him alive? Here I am worried about a Foley catheter, while Robert is worried about losing his house. I bet if Wayne had the option*

CHAPTER 10

of having to depend on a Foley to go to the bathroom or have his fingers and toes back, he'd choose the latter.

As I continue to deride my pessimism, I look over at Arnold, who's propped against the bed railing, and ask myself: *Why can't I be brave like a lion instead of scared like a mouse? Who am I to whine and complain when I know that Marty, Robert, or Wayne would trade places with me in a New York minute?* Without answering those rhetorical questions, I bring my pity party to an end.

My parents walk through the door just after six o'clock, and Daddy is eager to hear some good news. Although my statement is only partially true, I tell him that today, with help from Kim, I transferred from my wheelchair to a padded table.

"That's great! Any luck going to the bathroom yet?" he asks.

I respond, "No, but I can tell when my bladder is full." Despite the positive spin I put on my answer, I'm unable to hide the concern on my face, and Daddy sees it.

"You've come a long way, son. The Lord has been good to us. There's no need to worry. I mean it!" Daddy says. "How about Wendy's for dinner?"

"Sounds good," I reply.

As my dad walks to the door, Sharon shows up with two tennis rackets in her hand and a bright smile on her face.

Looking at Sharon, Daddy says, "I'm heading to Wendy's. Want anything?"

"No thanks. I ate before I left my apartment." Smiling at me, she asks, "Aren't you tired of Wendy's chicken sandwiches by now?"

"Yes, I am. . . . That's why I'm having a double cheeseburger!" I say with a smirk. "What's with the rackets?"

"I'm ready to challenge you to a volleying contest!" she exclaims.

"I don't think so," I reply bluntly. I want to share her enthusiasm, but I can't.

Sharon quickly picks up on my dejected mood. It's almost as if she was expecting this reaction from me. She kneels in front of my wheelchair and demands my attention. "Hey . . . look at me!" she commands. "It's just the two of us having fun. I don't need you to impress me."

"I can't do it," I say in a snippy tone.

"Can't or won't?"

"What does it matter?" I question in a raised voice.

"It matters to me!" she fires back. "If you physically *can't* do it, I can respect that. But if you won't even try because of your stupid pride then Houston, we have a problem!"

I look over at Mama and notice that she's quietly making her way out of the room. Sharon snatches a Nerf ball off my bed, takes the two rackets, tosses them in my lap, grabs the handles of my wheelchair, and makes a beeline for the door. I feel like I'm a fussy baby in a stroller and Sharon is a disgusted mother rushing me out of a restaurant. But I also realize that Sharon will never allow me to pity myself.

Sharon stops in front of the multipurpose room and locks the wheels to my chair. Putting a racket in her hand, she steps back several feet and glares at me.

I stare back at her for a couple seconds before quipping, "Houston, we have a problem? That's the best you could do?"

CHAPTER 10

"In the heat of the moment, yes." Her eyes brim with tears, but a slight smile sneaks across her face.

She walks over, kisses me, and tells me it's okay if I don't want to do this. I lie and tell her it'll be fun, even though hitting a ball with a racket is the last thing on earth I want to do.

Excited, Sharon steps back and gets ready to hit the Nerf ball to me. I wrap my left hand around the grip of the racket, then I look at the face of the racket as I twirl it in my hand. I stop and twirl it a second time and then a third.

"What are you doing?" Sharon asks, puzzled by my behavior.

"Watch the face of the racket," I say as I hold it outward toward her. I close my eyes and twirl the racket around several times then stop it with the face of the racket pointing at her.

At first, she has a perplexed look on her face, but just as I get ready to solve the mystery for her, she shouts, "You can feel your hand!"

"Yes!" I cheer. "The feeling is dull, but I can feel the panels of the grip." I tell her I'm baffled that I haven't noticed this feeling before.

"Thanks to me, now you know," she says boasting playfully.

As we hit the ball back and forth, the familiar mechanics of my stroke return. We can only produce a few volleys before I lose strength in my hand and arm, but it's a fun activity while it lasts.

When we return to my room, my parents are expecting two fighting catbirds to fly through the door. Instead, we greet them with smiling faces. While devouring a double cheeseburger, I share with my parents the discovery that I have some patchy feeling in my left hand and the ability to volley a Nerf ball. They couldn't be happier.

Just before seven, Mike Bousman drops by. He wants to know if I've had the urge to urinate yet. I tell him I can feel when my bladder is full, but I still can't get any urine to come out. He informs me that if the medicine doesn't stimulate my bladder by late tomorrow, then he has orders from Dr. Alsentzer to put in a Foley catheter. When he leaves, a hushed silence falls over the room.

Daddy walks over to me, kneels down, and says, "Worrying over this won't change a thing. Keep drinking and praying."

"I can't say I won't worry, but I realized today that I'm the fortunate one—with or without a Foley catheter."

Before leaving for home, Daddy and Sharon help me transfer to my bed. Sharon fills up my thermos, kisses me, and tells me to think positive thoughts.

As I lie in bed, my flesh and faith battle each other for hours. One minute, I'm convinced I'll have to use a catheter to urinate forever; the next minute, I believe the Lord will intervene and restore the use of my bladder.

Around one o'clock in the morning, James wakes me up. "Hey, brother. Any luck goin' to the bathroom?"

"I'm afraid not," I reply groggily.

"Do you have any juice left?" he asks.

"Yeah, on the rolling table behind you," I respond.

CHAPTER 10

"We're gonna try straight prune juice," he says. "Drink every drop. I'll see you at six."

I do as James tells me. By two, the thermos is empty, and I feel like I'm going to float away. I lie awake and push on my abdomen. I have the overwhelming urge to go, but I simply can't relax my bladder, and it's so frustrating! Visualizing how great it would feel to relieve myself, I stop pressing on my bladder and just take big deep breaths until I fall back asleep.

A couple hours later, I wake up because I think I'm going to the bathroom, but I soon realize I was only dreaming.

Like clockwork, James shows up at six. "Did the prune juice work?" he asks.

"Nope," I say, defeated.

Without responding, James places a sterile catheter and gloves on the bed and pulls back the covers. "Aw, man! You played me!" he hollers with a chuckle.

"What do you mean?" I respond, totally confused.

"Check this out, brother!" he says as he raises the head of my bed. There, between my legs, is a yellow spot the size of a beach ball.

"Yes!" I shout. "Thank you, Jesus!"

James and I high-five each other, then he asks, "When did you go?"

"I'm not sure," I admit. "At one point last night, I woke up because I *thought* I was peeing, but I convinced myself that I was just dreaming."

James mixes me another thermos of cranberry juice, prune juice, and ginger ale. This time, instead of cathing me, he places a urinal between my legs. Laughing, he tells me he'll stop by the nurses station and let someone know I wet the bed.

With a heavy dose of sarcasm, I thank him. Then, joking aside, I sincerely thank him for going above and beyond the call of duty for me. He shrugs off my gratitude and asks if I want to sit up or lie back down. Smiling, I tell him I want to sit up and admire our accomplishment.

Once James leaves, I stare down at the soiled sheets. I'm so grateful for this moment that I silently say a prayer of thanksgiving. I can't help but think I was hours away from being shackled with a Foley catheter and leg bag. Now I just have to put some urine in the bottom of this urinal, so I guzzle the thermos of James's concoction while I wait for a nurse to come by and get me cleaned up. While I wait, an idea pops into my head: *Wouldn't it be a funny surprise when Mama and Daddy arrive later today if I pull back the covers and reveal the soiled sheets!*

Shortly after seven, my good luck charm shows up. "So you peed on yourself," Althea says with a cackle.

"I sure did!" I respond gleefully.

"Well, congratulations. I know your parents will be *so* proud of you." You can cut her sarcasm with a knife.

"Speaking of my parents, what are the chances I can leave the sheets on the bed until they get here for visiting hours?"

Althea just stares at me with a blank expression for a couple of seconds. "Can you look out the window and see the wing attached to this building?" She points toward the window and continues, "That's the psychiatric ward, which is where

CHAPTER 10

you belong." She rolls her eyes and in a snarky tone says, "No, I will *not* keep these sheets on the bed so they can stink up the entire room."

"How 'bout this? You put clean sheets on the bed and leave behind the dirty fitted sheet. And for that, I'll give you a handful of peanut M&M's."

"Boy, you are gonna drive me to drink—not to mention get me fired!" she says.

"I have James's cocktail right here in my thermos if you need a drink," I counter, and we both crack up.

Althea provides me with a bowl of warm water, a washcloth, and soap so I can clean myself. James has left behind a sterile catheter in case I had no luck going into the urinal. Before getting me dressed, Althea notices that the urinal is still empty, which means she has the privilege of catheterizing me.

Once I'm dressed and sitting in my wheelchair, she takes the dirty sheets off the bed. I grab the soiled fitted sheet and place it in my hamper for safekeeping until I can show it to my parents. Then I wheel myself over to the dresser, grab my jar of M&M's, and present them to Althea as a peace offering.

"Drivin' me to drink *and* tryin' to make me fat too," she grumbles wearily.

"I love you, Althea," I respond, smiling from ear to ear.

"As well you should." After politely declining the M&M's, Althea puts a small paper cup in my hand with three pills in it. Then she walks across the hallway to take care of her next patient.

My Thursday morning continues to get better with a successful trek to physical therapy, where I transport myself from a distance of more than a hundred feet.

THE VIEWFINDER

During the first session of PT, I fully rotate the pedals of the stationary bike a handful of times. During the second session, I successfully stand on my left foot. Then, with minimal help from Kim, I pivot from a standing position to sit down on the padded table. I know this good news will put big smiles on Mama's and Daddy's faces tonight.

In occupational therapy, patients can choose to paint a ceramic vase or mug. I am putting my first coat of off-white paint on my mug, which will show the date of my accident and my release date from the rehab center. While working on it, I ask Brandy to explain the criteria used to determine when a patient is ready to go home.

"The short and simple answer is when the rehab staff determines that a patient has attained the skills needed to take care of themselves. But things in the rehab center are rarely straightforward," she informs me.

"How about if a person isn't able to acquire the skills to take care of themselves? What then?" I ask.

"It depends on several factors, but a lot of our older patients—the ones who don't develop the skills to take care of themselves—move into assisted-living facilities."

Her answer makes me wonder, *If I'm released from rehab and it's determined that I can't take care of myself, where will I go?* I'm still a long way from being able to take care of myself, and I can't expect my parents to take care of me. I mean, I'm a grown man—I'll be twenty-four this year—so it's a sobering thought.

At the end of OT, as the patients clean up their messes, I notice a driving

CHAPTER 10

simulator parked against the wall.

"Has that simulator always been there?" I inquire.

"No," Brandy replies. "We had to send it off to get recalibrated. We just got it back yesterday."

"What do you use it for?" I ask.

"We primarily use it to assess whether patients are physically ready to drive again."

Like a slap in the face, it hits me: I bet I have to complete a driving test again because of my injury. When I ask Brandy, her answer is yes. But not being able to drive doesn't bother me. I'm more worried about where I'll live after I leave this place and who's going to help take care of me.

After OT, Brandy wheels me back to my room for lunch. I've been drinking James's cocktail all morning, and, again, I feel like my bladder is full. Instead of having Charles cath me, I grab the urinal and wheel myself into the bathroom. I take some deep breaths, press my bladder, and wait. Just as I'm about to give up—splash down! The sweet sound of urine hitting the bottom of the urinal is music to my ears. I hide the half-filled urinal behind the toilet for safekeeping until I can show it to my parents. Going to the bathroom on my own may not be a sign of divine intervention, but it's certainly an answer to my prayers.

When I finish my lunch, I attend my session with Dr. Duncan and share the good news about emptying my bladder, rotating the pedals on the bike, and my success in transferring from my wheelchair to a padded table.

Although he's happy with my physical progress, he challenges my unwillingness to talk about the impact my injury has had on me psychologically, especially as it relates to tennis. I tell him again that I'm not ready to talk about the subject, but I do share with him that Sharon convinced me to put my pride aside, pick up a racket, and just try to have fun. Dr. Duncan considers that progress and stops pressuring me. I spend the rest of the session hooked up to the biofeedback machine and meditating.

When visiting hours roll around, I eagerly await my parents' arrival. I'm hopeful Sharon will show up too. I hang my urine-stained fitted sheet along the bed railing so that the yellow spot is front and center like a big smiley face. Then I wait for Mama and Daddy in the hallway outside my room.

Shortly before shift change at seven, I notice Althea chatting with a couple of nurses in the hallway. She's closer to the entrance to the rehab center than I am, so I'm worried she'll see my parents first and spoil my surprise.

Springing into action, I grab the hallway handrail and pull myself over to her. Because of the growing strength in my left arm and leg, I pull up next to Althea and the other nurses within a minute. "I'm sorry for interrupting, but can I speak to you in private?" I say to Althea.

She sighs heavily, frowns, and glares at me for a moment before resuming her conversation with her colleagues.

"Althea, please. I need to speak to you," I plead.

Again, she stares at me. Her eyes are like lasers. "Why are you still here?" she

CHAPTER 10

says as if I'm her annoying little brother. "Go away! Now!"

"Althea, if you see my parents, please don't tell them about the soiled sheets!" I beg.

The other nurses look at Althea in bewilderment. "What is he *talking* about?" one nurse asks incredulously.

"He doesn't know what he's talkin' about. Just ignore him," Althea snaps.

On my way back to my room, I realize how juvenile I must seem getting all excited about showing my parents a pee-stained sheet. When my parents arrive, their timing is perfect. Just as they turn the corner and head down the hall toward me, Althea steps inside another patient's room.

"Hey, Mackel! How you doing?" Daddy asks.

"I'm good. Go check out what's hanging across my bed," I say as I follow the two of them into my room.

"Did you do this?" Daddy asks excitedly after seeing the sheet draped across the bed railing.

"Yes, he did. Early this morning," Althea answers smugly.

I turn to see her standing in the doorway to my room. For a moment, I'm upset that she stole my thunder, but then I tell my parents that thanks to Althea, I'm able to show this beautifully soiled sheet to them.

Daddy looks at Althea and asks her if I offered her any of my get-well pills to say thank you. She chuckles and tells him I did but explains that my special healing pills are going to make her fat. Then she looks at me and smiles.

THE VIEWFINDER

Althea chats with my parents for a few minutes before announcing that she's off the clock and ready to go home. Before walking out the door, she grabs the dirty sheet and takes it with her. I go into the bathroom, retrieve my half-filled urinal, and emerge with it hooked to the armrest of my wheelchair. Then I hold it up like a championship trophy, show it to my parents, and announce that it has been a banner day.

I explain that James played a pivotal role in making this happen last night and early this morning, but the three of us also believe that the good Lord played the most significant role in allowing me to regain the use of my bladder. Coupled with the successes I had during physical therapy, Thursday, January 16, has truly been a blessed day for me and my family.

CHAPTER 11

BY JANUARY 22, I have made significant strides in my recovery. Over the past few days, the right side of my body, notably my right leg, has shown a lot of improvement. Now, with both of my feet strapped to the pedals of the old stationary bike, I can turn the crank arms of the bike fifteen to twenty times before getting tired. In full disclosure, my left leg is doing most of the work; my right leg is just along for the ride.

With help, I can also stand for almost thirty seconds before tiring. My left hand and arm are strong enough and coordinated enough to do all that's required of me in both physical and occupational therapy. However, since I still have very little function in my right hand, OT has fitted me with a glove that gives me enough traction on the wheel to push my chair forward and pull backward. Disappointingly, I still have to sit down to pee into a urinal. But that's about to change today.

I recall when, as a young boy, I enjoyed pulling down my pants and peeing, mostly on passing cars. I'm tired of asking a nurse to help me pull down my pants, sit, and use the urinal every time I have to go to the bathroom. Since I've been

THE VIEWFINDER

challenging myself to regain my autonomy in so many parts of my daily routine, I've decided that today is the day I will go into the bathroom, stand up, pull down my pants, and pee in the toilet like men do every day. I am confident that I can stand and urinate on my own because I can stand and hold myself up in physical therapy. The tricky part will be pulling down my spandex pants. I'll have to use my weak right hand since I need my left hand to hold on to the safety rail for balance.

When I feel the urge to pee, I wheel my chair into the bathroom and situate myself in front of the toilet. As I'm facing the toilet, the handrail is on the left, which makes it easy for me to use the stronger side of my body to lift myself into a standing position. I tell myself, *You have thirty seconds to stand, pull down your pants, and go to the bathroom.* In my head, I count to three, then I pull myself up to a standing position. With my right hand, I claw at my pants, pulling them down far enough to urinate. But it takes longer than I expected, so as I relieve myself, I can feel my left leg starting to fatigue. Even so, I say out loud, "You got this!" Unfortunately, those words barely leave my lips when my left leg collapses, and I drop like a sack of potatoes.

As I go down, my butt cheeks catch the front part of the wheelchair seat, and it acts as a catapult, thrusting me forward. The weight of my halo and vest sends my head straight into the toilet. The impact of the front rods of my halo hitting the inside of the toilet bowl produces excruciating pain, and I see stars for a couple seconds. When I try to lift my head out of the toilet, the tip of the front right rod catches underneath the rim of the toilet seat. Undeterred, I continue working to

CHAPTER 11

find a way out of this predicament but without success. My oh so graceful fall has left me on my knees with my head slightly turned to the left. Although my head is aching, I can't help but laugh at myself. I can add this debacle to the long list of my life's most embarrassing moments!

The comical aspect of my fall quickly wears off when I feel and see blood running down my eye and off my cheek into the toilet. Fortunately, I'm able to reach over and pull the cord to call for help.

"Yes?" the nurse calls over the intercom.

"Hey, I need help in the bathroom," I say.

"Hello? Do you need something?" she asks again.

Apparently, having my head in the toilet bowl muffles the sound of my voice, so at the top of my lungs, I shout, "Yes! I'm stuck in the bathroom and need help!"

"Are you locked in the bathroom?" she asks, trying to clarify my response.

"No, I've fallen and can't get up!"

"Okay, someone will be right there."

As I wait for some help, my legs, which are pinned underneath me, start to spasm. Each spasm pushes my body forward, jamming the rod further against the toilet bowl. The pain is agonizing. Although life has ordered up a large portion of pain at this moment in time, I'm forced to enjoy an even bigger piece of humble pie when the nurse knocks on the bathroom door.

"What *happened*?" she asks in a perplexed voice.

"Don't laugh, but my head is stuck in the toilet," I mutter, feeling completely humiliated. Not only is my head stuck in the toilet but my naked butt is on full display.

Mystified, the nurse asks, "How did this happen?"

"I was standing up going to the bathroom, and my legs gave out," I reply.

Leaning down to help me up, she sees the blood on my face and in the toilet and immediately pulls the call button. "I need help in 116 *stat*."

Two nurses show up within seconds. Working together, they carefully extricate my head and halo from the toilet without injuring me further. Once I'm back in the wheelchair, they check out my pin sites. Only the one on the front right is bleeding.

Adding to my embarrassment, someone has contacted Dr. Alsentzer, who shows up several minutes later. At his request, I recount how my head ended up in the toilet. Fortunately, instead of scolding me for my momentary lapse in judgment, he laughs at my misfortune. Then he gives me a pinprick test and orders a CAT scan of my head and neck, just to be safe.

He insists that I stay in bed until orderlies can take me to radiology. As a result, I miss my afternoon therapy sessions. Finally around four o'clock, the orderlies arrive and take me down to radiology. The CAT scan shows my neck is still in alignment and only the right pin needs tightening; the other three remain secure in my skull.

It's after five when I return from radiology, and my parents are waiting in my room. When I give them a play-by-play of my swan dive into the toilet bowl, they find nothing funny about my reckless bathroom venture. But when my brother shows up a little while later, he finds it hilarious.

CHAPTER 11

Late the following Saturday afternoon, the laughs between my brother and me soar to another level. Weekends at the rehab center are bustling and full of activity since many family members come to visit patients. As soon as Lee walks into my room, he bends over laughing so hard he can hardly catch his breath. When he stands up, the first thing I notice is the supersize, red velvet bowtie around his neck, which matches his ruby-red face. After taking in his entire ensemble, I realize that my brother has transformed himself into a flamboyant doctor. Lee saunters by my bed like a runway supermodel, making exaggerated turns and striking poses, which, of course, makes me laugh. Underneath the bowtie, he's sporting a red-and-yellow plaid polyester shirt with a flyaway collar large enough to land a small plane. His burgundy double-knit bell-bottom pants are three inches too short, which shows off his yellow argyle socks and brown penny loafers. The high-water effect of his pant legs is due in part to the fact that the waistline of his trousers is several inches above his navel. In addition, the brown leather belt holding up his pants is several inches too long, producing what looks like a tongue dangling down from his waist, which only increases the outrageousness of the outfit. For a last touch of authenticity, Lee has somehow gotten his hands on a white lab coat and a stethoscope that's hanging around his neck.

Lee suggests that we go have some fun, so he helps me out of bed and into my wheelchair, then we mosey down the main hallway that connects the rehab center to the hospital. A few people scrutinize us with curious stares, then about halfway down the hall, we cross paths with two nurses.

"Good afternoon, ladies," Lee greets.

"Hello, doctor," one of them responds, and we both start giggling.

Lee pulls my chair to an abrupt stop and walks in front of me like a penguin. His pants are pulled up so high that he's given himself an atomic wedgie. When we get to the hospital lobby, we join several other people waiting for the elevator. The doors open, and Lee and I wait as the elevator empties one load of passengers and picks up another.

Once we're inside the elevator, Lee kneels down and places the stethoscope on my chest. "Sir, take a few deep breaths for me," he says with concern in his voice. Lee moves the scope to different places on my chest, each time asking me to take a deep breath. Hilariously, no one seems to notice that the stethoscope is on the outside of my hard, plastic vest.

"This is not good," Lee says out loud, shaking his head. Then he directs his attention to a woman standing next to the elevator control panel. "Excuse me, ma'am," he says as he taps the lady on the shoulder. "Will you push L4, stat, for the cardiology floor?"

When he says the word *stat*, I snicker but quickly turn my suppressed laughter into a moan of discomfort.

Hearing a doctor request the cardiology floor, the people in the elevator take a step back as if to give him some room in case his patient goes into cardiac arrest. Doing my best to play the part of a distressed patient, I begin fake-coughing to cover up my giggles.

CHAPTER 11

When the elevator doors open to the second floor, there's a mass exodus. No one gets on the elevator, and the doors close. We ride to the next floor, gasping for air as our laughter fills the elevator. While it may seem somewhat shameful for two grown men to traipse around the hospital like mischievous adolescents, for half an hour, my brother helps me forget the seriousness of my new normal as a person with quadriplegia. Eventually our fun ends, and Lee takes me back to my room and helps me get into bed. After that, Dr. Bowen heads back to Washington, never fully understanding the healing power of his visit.

Early on the morning of Monday, January 27, I resume my daily regimen of activity, determined as ever to achieve my goals. I've gradually been increasing the distance I travel to therapy every morning, and today is the day I've designated to wheel myself from my room all the way through the doors of the physical therapy center. The good news is that I can now use my left leg and a little of my right one to push and pull my wheelchair.

As I make my way down the hall, I greet most staff members by name. They recognize me because of my outfit and the fact that I carry two tennis rackets with me in a book bag draped over my chair, just in case anyone is interested in a friendly game of "hallway tennis." The object of the game is to volley the Nerf ball back and forth without allowing the ball to touch the floor.

Halfway through my journey to physical therapy, Jim Barrett stops and says hello. "Hey, I have about five minutes for a rematch," he says.

THE VIEWFINDER

"Let's do it!" I respond.

Jim reaches in my bag and pulls out my rackets and the Nerf ball. We hit the ball back and forth for a few minutes and enjoy some friendly competition. When we finish, Jim asks if I'm still up for some Ping-Pong on Thursday night, explaining that a few patients and staff in the psychiatric ward are holding a round-robin tournament. I hesitate at first but tell him I'll be there. Smiling, he turns and continues on his way down the hallway, and I make my way to PT.

At quarter past eight, I reach the front entrance of the physical therapy room. I'm excited to have achieved my goal and pleased with the fact that I'm not terribly tired. Clearly, my late-night workouts have paid off. Looking behind me, I take a moment to admire the evidence of my efforts: the multitude of scuff marks left on the baseboards that line the corridor.

As is customary at the start of the first PT session, Kim straps my feet to the pedals of the stationary bike. Shortly into my workout, an aide pushes a small boy in a wheelchair through the front doors of the facility. Based on his size, I guess that he's seven or eight years old. He's on his way to the burn center, which is adjacent to physical therapy. As he passes by me, I only see his eyes. A ski mask made of a neoprene-type material covers his face and neck, while his arms and legs are wrapped in sterile gauze.

Seeing his jovial demeanor, I suspect this is his first visit to the chemical sink tank. I wonder if he knows the pain that awaits him behind the door he's getting ready to enter. I have watched several burn patients enter the room and, minutes

CHAPTER 11

later, heard them scream in agony as therapists peel away layers of damaged skin. My heart breaks for the small boy, and I wish I could lend him my viewfinder or somehow put him in a deep sleep filled with images of comfort and safety. I say a silent prayer that God wraps his loving arms around the little boy and whispers brave thoughts in his ear. Sometimes life just isn't fair.

During the second session of PT, I ask Kim if she knows anything about the young burn victim. She tells me he was airlifted to Pitt County Memorial Hospital two weeks ago after a space heater in his bedroom caught fire in the middle of the night. I look at her and ask if the tragic stories that pass in and out of these doors ever become too much for her to handle.

"Yes, especially when it involves children," she says. "However, some tragic beginnings have happy endings, and that's what sustains me."

During PT and OT, I can't stop thinking about this little boy. *His disfiguring burns will be with him for the rest of his life. What are the chances that he won't get picked on in school by another Michael Bowen? Will he allow the cruelty of people to dictate his happiness, or will he be able to rise above their heartlessness? What will be his destiny?*

While I'm eating lunch, I allow these disheartening thoughts to turn inward as I wonder about my predicament. *What does my future hold? Before my accident, I had professional goals to become a tennis pro and teach others the game I love. Or maybe a career as a college tennis coach or a phys ed teacher awaited. The point is that I had goals before my accident. Now my future is a blank canvas. I can only have faith that God has my future goals mapped out for me.*

Living by faith is difficult. In fact, it's too scary for most people. But I'm not most people. I'm not the same person who pulled out in front of that car a couple months ago. I might be broken physically, but my spirit is whole, and it has transformed my heart. *Is this the work of the Holy Spirit?* I wonder. *I have no other explanation but to believe it is.*

While I languished in my car, seriously injured and desperately waiting for help, did God send a guardian angel to rescue me from my emotional despair? I believe he did. I believe Gramma was right all those years ago when she said we all have a guardian angel.

When I think back on those frightening moments, I believe a spiritual intervention took place. It wasn't a mere coincidence that Dr. Hatcher happened upon my accident to comfort me during this life-altering moment in my life. The images of my past seen through the lens of my viewfinder comforted me, protected me, and taught me a spiritual lesson in empathy. Recalling my cruel interactions with Annie and Trey infused my soul with an empathy toward others that, before my accident, did not exist. This newfound empathy is allowing me to feel compassion every day for other patients roaming these hallways. But in terms of the images of my future—my vision of me working out in physical therapy—the logical part of my brain tells me that, more than likely, Kim planted those pictures in my mind when she visited me during our early therapy sessions when I was still in the hospital.

CHAPTER 11

During my scheduled appointment with Dr. Duncan, I finally open up and share with him the details of my accident, including my interpretation of the images and dreams. Fearing the worst, I'm thankful when he just listens intently and doesn't diagnose me with some sort of delusional psychosis. Instead, he's intrigued by my description of the events that took place during those critical moments following my accident. He doesn't agree or disagree with my conclusions, and I'm grateful that he's not judgmental of my spiritual beliefs. The session passes so quickly that I'm surprised when his next patient knocks on the door, signaling that our time has expired.

Later that afternoon, patients congregate in the multipurpose room where Jim has organized a game of bingo for recreational therapy. The jackpot for winning a game is a snack-sized Snickers bar, which is my second-favorite candy after peanut M&M's. I'm surprised at how competitive the patients are—they seem desperate to declare victory and fill their mouths with miniature candy bars.

After bingo, Jim announces that this Friday is Italian Night Out, so we'll be taking a van to a local pizza parlor. Anyone who wants to go should meet in the lobby at five-thirty. While several patients verbally welcome the opportunity to eat something other than hospital food, my first thought is, *I'm not going out in public with bolts sticking out of my skull.*

As I'm returning to my room, I see a new guy in the hallway, so I stop and introduce myself. His name is Lenny, and he's lying on a bed, flat on his stomach. This is his first day at the rehab center. Curious, I ask him why he's lying

THE VIEWFINDER

facedown. He explains that a severe pressure sore on his rear end has landed him at the rehab center for treatment. Wondering how he made his way down the hallway, I soon notice that his narrow bed has tall wheels in the front like a wheelchair and small caster wheels in the back that allow him to maneuver the bed like a wheelchair.

I invite Lenny into my room for a friendly game of H-O-R-S-E. When we enter, I hear Mike playing his harmonica behind the curtain to his side of the room. Lenny checks out my backboard and compliments the design. I tell him the credit goes to my brother. While we're shooting hoops, Mike comes out from behind the curtain, so I introduce them. "Lenny, this is my roommate, Mike Hamer." The two of them shake hands.

I ask Mike to play us a couple tunes while we finish up our game, so he plays a few bars but then stops. Apparently, curiosity has gotten the best of him, too, because he asks Lenny why he's lying facedown on the bed. Lenny tells Mike about his bedsore but also mentions he has spina bifida and is usually wheelchair-bound. When Mike asks Lenny where he lives, he tells us just outside Greenville in an assisted-living facility. Hearing this, I immediately wonder if I'll be joining him when I'm released from rehab.

Lenny also shares with us that his passion is drawing. He produces a small sketch pad from underneath the bedsheet and shows us some of his work. I suspect the dark themes of his pencil sketches reflect his life experiences.

Mike and I share our stories of how we got injured, and Lenny gets a kick out

CHAPTER 11

of my willingness to dress up like a transvestite for money. I insist that it was not one of my finer moments. Lenny visits a while longer, and I feel like he's savoring the company, but after a couple of awkward lulls in our conversation, he says it's time to head back to his room for dinner.

After Lenny leaves and Mike returns to his side of the room to continue mastering the harmonica, I just sit and contemplate my future, wondering, *What will my new talent be now that my tennis career is over?*

THE VIEWFINDER

CHAPTER 12

Thursday is Ping-Pong night in the psychiatric ward, and true to his word, Jim Barrett invites me to join him. On the way there, I tease, "So tell me, will I feel like I'm in a scene from *One Flew Over the Cuckoo's Nest?*"

Jim chuckles and says, "Actually, you'll be hard-pressed to distinguish between staffers and patients. Most of the patients who take part are schizophrenic or bipolar and are having trouble managing their meds."

When we reach the recreational therapy room, the tournament has already started, so Jim and I sit and watch the action. There are two Ping-Pong tables and six players—five guys and a girl. Watching them play, I realize Jim was right. If two of them weren't wearing badges pointing out that they were staff members, I wouldn't be able to tell who's who.

Turning to me, Jim asks, "Did you grow up playing Ping-Pong?"

"Yep. I actually played a couple days before my accident. My doubles partner, Terry Gratz, and I frequented the student union at UNCW to look for people to

CHAPTER 12

play for cash."

Jim laughs and says, "You . . . a con man?"

"I'm afraid so," I reply. Then I explain to Jim that there were four keys to our success: The first one, of course, was to lose early. Second, while losing, we'd compliment our opponents. Next, we'd act like rookies. One of our common tricks was to fill a front pocket with tissue paper and hang part of a twenty-dollar bill out of it to make it look like we were suckers and easy to take advantage of. Finally, when we did win, we'd be sure to play it off as sheer luck with statements like, "I've never played this well in my life!" or "Usually, my ball can't even *find* the table!" And of course, the clincher, "Just watch, the next game you'll skunk me!"

The teams are only playing to eleven points, so the games don't last long. Since there are eight of us, it's decided that we'll play doubles, so Jim and I team up and join the next round. Because I'm in a wheelchair, we change the rules. Typically, in table tennis doubles, you and your partner have to alternate hitting the ball. Since I'm unable to quickly maneuver my chair around the table, we decide that if the ball lands on your half of the table, it's your ball. Therefore, a player can hit the ball multiple times in a row as long as the ball lands on that player's side.

During the brief warm-up, I soon realize that I'm at a disadvantage because it's much more difficult to hit the ball sitting down than it is standing up. Although I do my best to volley back and forth, I realize our opponents are taking it easy on me. I enjoy myself, but for the first time, I'm aware of how people without disabilities will treat me differently. Here, the other players are sensitive to my challenges. But it makes me wonder, *How will I feel when people act just the opposite and are unkind to me because I'm different?*

I get my answer to that question the following night when, at my parents' urging, I join several other spinal cord injury patients for the Friday night pizza outing. I show up just past five thirty and wait in the main lobby of the rehab center with Marty, Mike, Sandy, and Robert for the van to arrive. When the van pulls under the entryway just before six, we make our way through the sliding glass doors to find Jim standing by the van, lowering the hydraulic wheelchair lift that will hoist us into the vehicle.

Gazing at the group, I decide that who gets the most stares at the restaurant will be a toss-up between me with my halo or Marty with his chin-controlled wheelchair. Not only am I uneasy about being seen in public but also with every intersection we pass through, my body tenses up. Most likely, it's PTSD from getting T-boned at an intersection. The one enjoyable part of the ride is seeing familiar scenery. As a teenager, Lee and I and our friends often made the twenty-mile trek from Washington Park to Greenville to shop and enjoy the bands that played downtown.

When we arrive at the pizza place, the parking lot is full. *Great—a full house,* I complain to myself. *My nightmare is about to come true.* As the van pulls into a parking space next to the restaurant, I look through the windshield and see the sign for handicapped parking. It's a visible reminder that this spot is reserved for those less fortunate. I'm first to exit the van, and as I do, a little boy leaving the restaurant

CHAPTER 12

runs over, intrigued by the motion of the hydraulic lift lowering me to the sidewalk.

"Hello there," Jim says to the boy as he stands watching.

"Hey," is all the boy says, preoccupied with the movement of the lift.

The platform lowering me from the van comes to a rest on the asphalt. The boy's mother, who by now is standing next to him, grabs his hand as I roll off the platform toward them. The youngster's eyes move upward from the lift to my wheelchair then eventually fixate on my halo.

"What's that thing on your head?" he asks.

His mother leans down and says in a low voice, "Sweetie, it's not nice to ask that."

"It's okay," I reply. "It's called a halo."

Puzzled, he asks, "Why do you wear it?"

"I have to wear it because I hurt my neck."

"Caleb," his mother says impatiently, "we have to go. Daddy is waiting for us in the car." With one hand holding a pizza box, she pulls him toward the car with her other hand, and the two of them dart away.

I watch as Jim continues to operate the lift, lowering Mike, then Sandy, Robert, and Marty. Jim pushes me inside the restaurant and the others follow. Mike, Sandy, and Robert don't need his help since they have the use of their arms and hands and can easily manage their chairs, as can Marty in his powered wheelchair.

"You handled that situation with the little boy perfectly," Jim leans forward and whispers in my ear.

Once we're all inside the restaurant, the hostess greets us. After Jim tells her we have a reservation, she grabs a handful of menus and we follow her through the crowded restaurant. The loquacious atmosphere abruptly changes as our wheelchair choo-choo train travels to its destination. Some people smile at us; others see us and quickly glance away.

The staff has already put together a few tables for us and removed the chairs. But before we can get settled, Robert's legs start spasming without warning. He has been suffering from these involuntary spasms since the onset of his injury six weeks ago. Medication does little to ease the contractions or the pain. As his legs violently shake and squeeze together, expletives quietly roll off his tongue. Robert places his forearms between his legs while Jim grabs a metal wedge from a backpack hanging from the wheelchair. Jim places the metal wedge between Robert's spastic legs, preventing them from causing him further injury.

The spasms stop as abruptly as they started but not before the table of four sitting across from us witnesses the episode. From the baffled looks on their faces, I can tell they are clueless about what just happened. After a few whispers to each other, the group returns to eating dinner.

I feel bad for Robert. It's definitely not the kind of attention he wanted; it's not what any of us want. The incident makes me painfully aware that I'm now disabled—someone whom a person without a physical disability might pity. This feeling is exactly the reason I didn't want to go out in public.

When the server arrives to take our order, it's pizza all around. Mike asks Jim to reach into his satchel and pull out his adaptive cuffs that fit around his clawlike

CHAPTER 12

hands and allow him to hold eating utensils. As I watch this exchange, I realize that I forgot to bring *my* adaptive cuffs, so I'll need Jim to help me eat.

I'm ashamed to admit that I find comfort in knowing Marty can't feed himself either. Although we share this commonality tonight, my hands are becoming more and more functional, and with practice, I'll eventually be able to feed myself. Marty will not. I can move all my limbs; he can move none. I can only imagine the courage it takes for Marty to live each day. I'm not sure I could do it if I were in his shoes.

While we wait for our food, I notice a couple with two young children to my left. The boy looks about seven or eight; the girl is a toddler. The mother is trying to carry on a conversation with her husband, while the little girl is squirming to get out of her high chair. Both parents are oblivious to their son, who is looking at me and moving his upper body back and forth, mimicking my robotic movements. I tell myself that he's just a kid being a kid, but his mocking is demeaning just the same.

I turn away from the boy and stare straight ahead. I have a powerful feeling it's no coincidence that I'm experiencing this moment. Yet again, I believe the Lord is using this opportunity to teach me a lesson in empathy. This time it's not with the images in my viewfinder showing me making fun of Annie and Trey; instead, I'm on the receiving end of someone picking on me because I look different. Although the teasing is brief and inflicted by a small boy who probably doesn't know any better, it still hurts.

When our pizzas arrive, Jim makes Marty and me feel like it's his honor to hand-feed us rather than a chore. His selflessness is something I admire tremendously.

THE VIEWFINDER

My girlfriend, Sharon, has that same quality.

The pizza is delicious and a welcome reprieve from hospital food. It even trumps a Wendy's chicken sandwich. We all enjoy some lively conversation, and before we know it, it's after eight and time to return to the rehab center.

On the ride back, I reflect on my encounters with the two boys. The young boy who asked the curious questions about my halo didn't bother me at all. I welcomed his curiosity, and he learned something about me. Conversely, the little boy who mocked me learned nothing about me. Instead, he made me feel self-conscious and painfully aware of my disability as if I'm less of a person. Because they were autistic, I don't know if Trey or Annie experienced the same feelings I'm having now, but I know with certainty that my antics did cause them great distress. I realize bad karma can be a blessing when you fully understand why you're being subjected to its repercussions. Tonight's experience is a lesson in compassion and benevolence that I will remember for the rest of my life.

The first few days of February are routine. During a group meeting with Dr. Duncan, the topic is complex: developing coping skills to assist us in dealing with the life-altering changes to our bodies, our family dynamic, and the future. Lately, when I'm in PT and group therapy, I experience these brief bouts of survivor's guilt. I feel guilty because I'm the "lucky one" in the group, meaning that I entered rehab almost a complete quadriplegic and now I can stand and move both of my arms. When I look at Marty or Mike, I think, *That could, or maybe even should,*

CHAPTER 12

be me. With spinal cord injuries, a millimeter can mean the difference between a Michael Bowen and a Marty Silverstone. Sadly, I believe neither Marty nor Mike will ever walk again without some divine intervention. As a result, during group therapy I'm reluctant to talk about how my injury will alter my life because I hope that one day I *will* walk again, but I know others won't.

Fortunately, the guilt I feel diminishes when I listen to others in the group talk about their plans for the future. Mike Hamer tells us he's going to resume producing music with his band again. Lenny has his art, and Marty is going back to school to become a substance abuse counselor. I realize these guys have goals; *I'm* the one with no plan. Learning to walk again is an awesome goal, but it's not a plan for what I'm going to do with my life. As if he can read my mind, Dr. Duncan turns his attention to me and asks, "Michael, you rarely say much during these sessions. What are your plans once you leave the rehab center?"

I take a moment to formulate my answer before I speak. "My future is a blank. . . . Before my accident, I planned to earn a degree in phys ed and maybe someday become a college coach or a teaching tennis pro. But now my plans are like ripe apples in a basket—breaking my neck is the one apple that spoiled the bunch." As I scan the room, I notice everyone is looking down to avoid my gaze. To add to my despair, I confess that I feel guilty for regaining movement in my legs while others have not and that I consider myself the fortunate one in the group because I may someday walk again.

Thankfully, at that moment, Mike Hamer breaks the tension in the room.

THE VIEWFINDER

"The way you pedal that bike in physical therapy, maybe you'll ride a bicycle for a living," he quips. His witty comment produces laughs all around, and it's just what the doctor ordered.

I leave group therapy questioning my motto of taking one day at a time without focusing on the future. *Maybe I need to start thinking about my long-term plans as a person with quadriplegia!* Whether he meant to or not, Dr. Duncan has planted a looming question in my mind: *What am I going to do with the rest of my life?* There's no chance I can go back to school and finish my degree. Hell, I can't even hold a pencil in my right hand, let alone write with it.

It's quiet in the hallway that leads out of the multipurpose room where we hold group therapy. I'm in no rush to get back to my room, so I park my wheelchair—along with my gloomy outlook—in front of the large plate glass panels that line the hallway. Staring outside, I contemplate what my future holds. As I sit quietly, I pray, *Heavenly Father, open my eyes, my mind, and my heart so that I may be attentive to what your plans are for my future.* Then I just stare through the window, watching a squirrel hide acorns in a nearby flower bed.

With the help of a full belly from lunch and the thermal heat coming off the window, I doze off sitting upright in my wheelchair. While I'm asleep, I have a bizarre dream that I'm pedaling the gray stationary bike from the physical therapy room down a country road! I guess anything is possible in your dreams. Cruising alongside me are a couple of neighborhood kids on their bicycles. Off to my right, an elderly couple sits on their wraparound front porch. They wave hello, and I wave

CHAPTER 12

back. The sweet scent of drying tobacco fills the air. Intuitively, I know that I'm on a mission to bicycle across the country to motivate patients who have sustained spinal cord injuries.

When I wake up from my dream, I'm disoriented, but the tickle of fresh drool dripping down my chin promptly clears my head. I look at my watch and realize I've been asleep for almost forty-five minutes, so I wheel myself back to my room where I sit and try to make sense of my dream. *Is bicycling across the country God's answer to my prayer? If it is, he sure didn't waste any time getting back to me!*

For a fleeting moment, the thought of such an adventure fills me with anticipation, but more rational thoughts soon follow. *It wasn't a prescient vision that my viewfinder produced; it was nothing more than a dream manifested from Mike's comment during group therapy,* I convince myself. *Forget the dream and get back to the reality of figuring out what you're going to do when you leave this place.*

THE VIEWFINDER

CHAPTER 13

THE MONTH OF FEBRUARY can be quite cold in eastern North Carolina; however, this winter has been unseasonably warm. The temperature in the afternoons has reached the mid-fifties, and patients are venturing outside to the rehab center's courtyard. I enjoy the outdoors, but for me, the hotter the weather, the better. So, except for a few minutes during my transport to Greenville and going out for pizza, I have spent the last two months inside. Dr. Alsentzer has given me permission to go outside for an hour in the afternoons, but I'm fearful that I will somehow catch pneumonia again, even though I know breathing in cold air did not cause me to get sick.

On Saturday, February 8, when I tell my parents I'd like to eat lunch in the courtyard, they're all for it. Daddy makes a quick road trip to Parker's Barbecue, a restaurant that's well known in Pitt County for its pork BBQ. Since we'll be eating outside, I ditch my running tights for a pair of sweatpants. With the addition of a coat, beanie, and scarf, I'm ready for subzero temperatures.

In the courtyard, we gather around a concrete table and bench and enjoy our

CHAPTER 13

lunch. For a homegrown southerner, the taste of a good pork barbecue and slaw sandwich is second only to fried chicken. After lunch, I position my chair with my face directly into the sun, close my eyes, and soak in some rays.

After a few minutes of silence, Daddy says, "We've come a long way, Mackel."

"Yes, we have, Daddy."

Daddy's words are so true. Not only has our relationship come a long way, but my recovery has also been a family journey. I stop sunbathing, roll my chair next to Mama and Daddy, and say, "I have a confession to make to both of you." Concerned, Daddy's eyebrows move closer together. "My accident has changed me; it's changed the way I feel about myself and the two of you."

"It's changed all of us, son," Daddy replies.

"Maybe, but you don't understand. Before my accident, I called you guys collect from school every Sunday night just to check in and ask for money."

Mama interjects, "We just wanted to make sure you were okay."

"I know you did, Mama, and *I* just wanted to make sure I asked for money," I shamefully admit. "What I'm trying to tell you both is, I had countless times on the phone to say 'I love you' and 'Thank you for all the sacrifices you've made,' but I neglected to do so, and I'm so sorry!"

"Honey, there's no need to apologize," Mama says with a look of surprise on her face.

Before either of them can change the subject, I acknowledge that it has taken an accident—an accident that almost ended my life—to discover a love for them

THE VIEWFINDER

I didn't know existed inside me. Having completed my confessional, we move inside to warmer temperatures.

As is usual on Saturdays, the lobby is busy with family members coming to visit their loved ones, so Mama and I sit and people-watch. Daddy, never knowing a stranger, canvasses the lobby looking for someone to chat with. It's easy to see where I get my introverted personality, and it's not from my dad! When the lobby traffic thins out, I thank my parents for lunch and insist they go home. Once they exit the lobby doors, a sense of relief envelops me because now my parents truly know just how much I love them.

I return to a quiet room. Mike's bandmates have taken him on an afternoon excursion, so I take advantage of the solitude and read a few Bible verses Sharon earmarked for me in preparation for our Bible study in the morning. In the book of Ecclesiastes, I discover a verse that brings me comfort and helps answer the ever-present question I've tried to suppress: why did this happen to me? It reads, "When times are good, be happy; but when times are bad, consider this: God has made the one as well as the other. Therefore, no one can discover anything about their future." (Eccles. 7:14)

To me, the verse says, why *not* me? God has given us the free will to make our own choices in life. On November 19, 1985, I chose to blindly cross that intersection, and in doing so, I failed to see an oncoming car. As a result, I'm experiencing the "bad times" that came with my choice. I also believe that God uses his divine will to work in and through our life choices for his purposes. What frightens me

CHAPTER 13

is not knowing what his purpose for me is when I leave the rehab center. What will my destiny be as a disabled man?

After two months here, the rehab center feels like home. I'm self-sufficient and no longer need help getting in or out of bed, going to the bathroom, or dressing myself. Staffers know that in the evenings they might find me roaming the hallways looking for someone to play tennis or join me for a friendly game of H-O-R-S-E in my room. Remaining true to my goal, I am busy rebuilding my body from sunup to sundown.

On February 11, I really see my work ethic paying dividends. As is my custom, I show up for the first session of PT with plans to work out on my own, but Kim tells me she wants me to lay off the stationary bike today. I figure she wants me to save my leg strength for transferring back and forth from my chair to the padded table, so I spend the first session lifting light weights, working with resistance bands, and stretching. As the first session of PT winds down, Kim walks by and tells me to meet her at the parallel bars.

"What's up?" I ask. "What are we doing today?"

"*We* are not doing anything, but *you* are going to take your first step today!" she says assuredly.

Immediately, my heart rate increases, my breathing quickens, and the muscles in my neck and shoulders tighten. These physiological changes are familiar to me because I've experienced them many times on the tennis court during a close match.

"Are you up for this?" she asks cautiously.

"I got this," I respond with confidence, even though I know I've whispered those words under my breath in close matches and still lost.

Hearing my certainty, Kim positions my wheelchair between the parallel bars, locks the wheels, and removes the footrests from my chair. Hanging over one of the chrome bars is a safety belt. Kim grabs it and places it under my arms and around my chest. Reaching up from my wheelchair, I put my forearms on the bars. Then Kim counts to three and helps lift me to my feet. Dan, one of the other physical therapists, unlocks my chair and is ready to push it underneath me if necessary.

Once on my feet, I'm unsteady and extremely top-heavy. I grab a bar with my left hand, but my right hand won't cooperate. It's clenched in a fist, so Dan reaches around and forces my fingers away from my palm. Once I'm able to get a better grip, I use both arms to balance myself. I look over Kim's shoulder into the mirror and get a glimpse of myself. I can't see my legs, but it's obvious that I'm standing. For the first time, I discover I have enough sensation to feel the pressure of the floor beneath my feet.

"Okay, I want you to put all your weight on your left foot and try stepping forward with your right," Kim instructs me.

Following her directions, I lean heavily on my left foot. Kim uses the safety strap to hold me firmly in place while I try moving my right foot forward. However, my leg is too weak to lift off the floor, so Kim has Dan take off my right shoe. With just my sock on, I slide my right foot forward and take my first step. Then she tells me to shift my weight to my right leg and try moving my left foot forward.

CHAPTER 13

When I do, my right leg trembles from fatigue, but before it buckles, I manage to slide my left foot forward a few inches.

Kim holds me up while Dan pushes the wheelchair underneath me. Exhausted, I collapse onto the seat. I rest my elbows on my thighs while holding the rods of my halo to keep me from toppling over onto the floor. Beside me, I hear Kim breathing hard, and suddenly, I'm overcome with emotion. Kim kneels in front of me, grabs my forearms, and says, "You have earned these two steps. I am *so* proud of you."

The tears streaming down my cheeks are not just tears of joy because I've taken my first steps. These are triumphant tears celebrating all my hard work. My effort and determination have literally allowed me to put one foot in front of the other. The weeks of pushing and pulling myself around the rehab center late at night, pedaling the stationary bike, and putting in the hard work during physical therapy have paid off.

At lunchtime, I contemplate calling my parents to give them the good news, but I decide to wait until I can tell them in person. When visiting hours begin, Sharon is the first to arrive. She finds me chatting with Mike and two members of his band.

"Hey there!" I say, grinning from ear to ear.

"What's up with the big smile?" she asks suspiciously as she looks at the faces around the room.

"Nothing's up," I fib. "I'm just happy to see you."

"You're a terrible liar," she retorts. She scans the room, looking at everyone as if we're all keeping a secret from her.

"Why don't we take a stroll around the rehab center, and I'll share this deep dark secret that I'm keeping from you," I suggest.

Sharon pushes my wheelchair just beyond the door of my room and kneels beside me. "I'm waiting," she says impatiently.

Laughing, I say, "You're *so* bossy!"

"Tell me now! It must be good news or you wouldn't be smiling."

Unable to hold it in any longer, I come clean. "I took my first steps today in physical therapy. Well, actually, they were more like shuffles than steps."

Sharon grabs both of my hands and clasps them together. With her lips to my hands, she closes her eyes and whispers, "Thank you, Jesus." Then she leans in and kisses me. Our kiss lingers, but neither of us care that we're in the middle of a busy hallway. Just before Sharon pulls away, we hear a familiar voice.

"No PDA in the hallway," Althea says sarcastically as she walks past us.

"No PDA?" Sharon repeats inquisitively.

"No public displays of affection," I clarify with a smirk. We both smile, guilty as charged.

Taking her position behind my wheelchair, Sharon pushes me toward the main lobby. While we wait there for my parents, Sharon grabs the rackets from my book bag and we volley back and forth. Over the past few weeks, we've improved, and our volleys now often exceed ten to fifteen hits.

CHAPTER 13

I notice that our game has drawn the attention of a small boy who is visiting his grandfather, and I can tell he's eager to play. "You wanna play?" I say, extending my racket toward him.

The young boy smiles and sheepishly grabs the racket. At first, he holds it with two hands like a baseball bat, so I show him how to properly hold it and choke up on the grip. Once he gets the hang of it, I keep one eye on their game and the other on the lobby entrance. Sharon is chasing down the Nerf ball when my parents walk in. My mom is carrying a familiar paper bag with an imprint of Wendy's iconic red pigtails and freckled face.

"Hey, Mackel. How ya doing?"

"I'm doing good, Daddy."

Just then, Sharon walks over and looks at me. "Did you tell your parents?" she asks.

"Tell us what?" Daddy says.

"Michael Bowen!" Sharon calls out. "Don't be a blockhead!"

"Oh yeah, I forgot to tell you. I stood up and took a couple of steps today in physical therapy," I say nonchalantly.

Daddy walks over to me, gets down on one knee, and says with tears in his eyes, "That is music to my ears, son. I'm so proud of you." My mom follows with a kiss on my forehead. This parental acknowledgment of a job well done is something every child craves. Unfortunately, as a child, I did little to nothing for my parents to be proud of. But at this moment, I realize it's never too late to achieve something to be proud of.

We sit in the lobby while I eat my dinner and share the details of taking my first steps. I mention that sometimes I feel guilty for being the "lucky one" in our group of patients with spinal cord injuries because I can move my legs, and now I've taken my first steps. My parents assure me that my feelings are perfectly natural. But I just want Mike, Marty, and the others to enjoy the same success I'm having.

Daddy looks at me and asks, "If the roles were reversed and you were sitting in Mike's or Marty's wheelchair, how would you feel about their success?"

"Less fortunate," I reply.

Shaking his head, Daddy says, "Stop feeling guilty and start feeling fortunate."

Considering the matter closed, my father changes the subject. "Sharon, how are your spring classes going at ECU?" he asks.

"Good. I'm really enjoying my sign language class," she replies.

When I finish my Wendy's dinner, we head back to my room. I hope Mike is there because Daddy enjoys his company. Unfortunately, we arrive to an empty room so the four of us spend the rest of the visit watching an episode of *The A-Team*.

Before heading home, Daddy combs my hair to one side and tells me he has to keep the minutes for Washington Park's board meeting tomorrow night, so he and Mama will see me on Thursday.

Sharon waits for my parents to leave before she kisses me and says good night. Before leaving, she reminds me that she'll be getting together with a group of her classmates the next couple of nights to study for a big test, so she'll see me on Friday.

The next day, I can't wait to make my way to physical therapy to see if I can

CHAPTER 13

reproduce my success on the parallel bars. When I show up, Kim has a surprise for me: a pair of ankle and foot orthotics (AFOs). These braces run underneath my feet, up the backs of my calves, and stop just shy of where my knees bend. She tells me they'll help with the drop foot I'm experiencing in both ankles.

As Kim straps on the orthotics, I notice she has lowered the parallel bars a few inches from where they were yesterday. She explains that it's so I can hold my arms in a locked position when I stand and grab the bars. She puts the safety strap around my chest and helps me stand, and I immediately notice that I'm more stable now that I can extend my arms. When Kim moves behind me, I finally get a clear view of my reflection in the large mirrors and see myself standing erect.

The first thing I see is my belly sticking out from underneath my vest. My chiseled stomach has disappeared! "Crap," I groan with disgust. "I used to have a nice six-pack. Now I look like I ate a bowling ball for breakfast."

Kim laughs and replies, "The cafeteria doesn't serve bowling balls."

"Ha. Not funny. I've gotta lay off the Wendy's and peanut M&M's."

Directly behind me, I feel Kim pulling up on the belt. She tells me to step first with my right foot and then my left. I lean forward enough to look down at my feet, shift my weight to the left, and take a heel-toe step with my right foot. Then I transfer my weight to my right side and take a step with my left foot. I take two additional steps before Kim grabs my wheelchair and I sit down. The AFOs are a game changer. Although I'm exhausted, I'm not an emotional mess like I was yesterday. And I feel confident that one day I *will* walk on my own.

THE VIEWFINDER

Just before I leave for OT, Kim tells me the rehabilitation team is meeting on Monday to discuss my discharge date. Upon hearing the word *discharge,* my heart sinks. I tell her pointedly, "I'm not ready to go home."

"Hold on. We're just meeting on Monday. The team may recommend you stay longer," she clarifies.

I don't ask the burning question on the tip of my tongue: what will *her* recommendation be? Irritated, I abruptly make my way to the OT room without saying goodbye. The bombshell Kim just dropped on me has taken away the jubilation I felt for taking those few steps.

In occupational therapy, I put a final coat of paint on my ceramic cup before stenciling on the date of my accident. While I paint, I get lost in thought about leaving this place. *Why am I upset over the possibility that they may discharge me sooner rather than later? Most patients can't wait to leave this place. Yeah, but those patients usually have husbands, wives, and children to go home to, and I don't. And some patients are discharged early because their insurance company stops paying for rehab, which to me is criminal. But even worse are the patients who waste their insurance company's money and the therapist's time by putting forth minimal to no effort during therapy.*

Before I know it, I've spent an hour dwelling on these negative thoughts. After therapy, I go back to my room for lunch, but I have no appetite. Althea peeks her head in the door and sees me staring at the floor. "Looks like somebody just lost his best friend," she says with a frown.

CHAPTER 13

"It feels that way," I say glumly.

"Okay, I'll bite. What's up?"

"Kim told me the rehab team is meeting on Monday to talk about my discharge date."

"That's great news! So why the sad face?"

"I'm not ready to leave this place! But I bet you're ready for me to leave because I'm a thorn in your side," I say.

"No, that's not true. If you recall, you were a pain in my *chest*!" she says with a grin and a chuckle.

"I'm not laughing, Althea!"

The smile disappears from her face as she squats down so she's eye level with me. "Outside these walls, a new reality is waiting for you. You're frightened of that and understandably so." After pausing for a moment, she continues, "I've been a nurse here for many years, and I have *never* seen a patient with more determination and self-discipline than you! When the team decides it's time for you to leave here, it's because you'll be ready."

After Althea's pep talk, I head to recreational therapy and then group therapy where I keep to myself. I can't shake the sobering thought of leaving the rehab center and moving on with my life. By the time evening sets in, I'm in no mood for company, so it's a good thing no one is stopping by to visit tonight. I can't even find the motivation to stay up and work out. The news of my impending discharge has put me in a funk.

I lie awake in bed asking myself, *Why am I so reluctant to leave this place?* Every reason I come up with leads me to the same conclusion: Althea is right; I'm afraid of what lies ahead for me. Now, as a quadriplegic, the unknown scares me despite my faith. Not knowing where I'll live scares me. Not having a plan for the future scares me. I feel comfortable inside the walls of this place. It has become my safe haven.

Once I leave these surroundings, I don't know how the outside world will treat me, and that scares me. There are some people who want to stand out and say, "Hey, look at me!" But I just want to blend in. These discouraging thoughts swirl around my mind like a whirlwind. I fall asleep praying to God that he will calm these worrisome thoughts. I ask him to strengthen my faith and help me find peace in whatever my future holds.

CHAPTER 14

On Thursday morning, I wake up with a somewhat better disposition. I tell myself, *No sulking today. Stay true to your motto: "All day long, do your very best, and let God worry about the rest."* Throughout the day, I do just that. During physical therapy, neither Kim nor I speak about my discharge date. I pedal the bike and put in my rep work on the weight machines, then, during the last part of my therapy session, I get hooked up to a TENS unit to help ease the ongoing pain in my right shoulder.

In occupational therapy, I spend ten to fifteen minutes pedaling an arm ergometer to strengthen my hands and arms. When I finish that, I work with the Fluidotherapy machine to increase the blood flow to my hands and increase my range of motion. Next, Brandy introduces me to a portable muscle stimulator. By placing the electrode pads on the muscles of my right forearm, the stimulator opens and closes my compromised hand. After she shows me where to place the pads, I sit in awe watching my hand open and close with absolutely no help from me.

THE VIEWFINDER

Late in the afternoon, I meet with Dr. Duncan and work with the biofeedback machine. When he asks me how I'm managing the guilty thoughts about my ability to move my legs while others cannot, I tell him that my dad has helped me develop a healthier perspective, which has increased my ability to cope.

"How so?" Dr. Duncan inquires.

"Simply put, my dad told me to stop feeling guilty and start feeling fortunate."

Nodding his head, Dr. Duncan says, "I couldn't have said it better myself. Your father is a wise man."

Dinner, visiting hours, and my parents all arrive at the same time. As is his custom, Daddy asks me if I have any good news. I tell him that Kim told me yesterday that the rehab team is meeting on Monday to determine my discharge date.

"That *is* good news!" Mama cries out.

"No, it's not!" I correct, shaking my head and shoulders. "I'm not ready to leave yet. I can't even take care of my most basic needs!"

"That's what we're here for, son—to take care of you," Daddy replies, trying to calm me.

"Are you guys okay with me moving back home?"

"Of course, we are!" Mama says incredulously, as if she couldn't imagine I would go anywhere else.

"Son, your mama and I have already met with the rehab coordinator about this, and we're in the process of making the house accessible for you. It's a done deal." Then, sensing this is something that's been weighing heavily on my mind, Daddy

CHAPTER 14

walks over to my wheelchair, leans down, and says, "You're coming home with us, and you will stay at home until you're ready to live on your own. Understood?"

My eyes fill with tears of gratitude, and I marvel at how fortunate I am to have parents who will raise me not once but twice! Physically, I'm a grown man, but I also feel like a small child once again because I'm unable to take care of myself. The difference this time is that I fully understand how unconditional their love for me is. Knowing that when I leave this place I'm going home with Mama and Daddy is the answer to my prayers.

On Monday, February 17, as I'm perched on the edge of the padded table, Kim says, "I want you to know that at the team meeting this afternoon, I'm going to recommend you be discharged at the end of the week."

Without saying a word, I transfer to my chair, put down my footrests, and wheel myself away.

Firmly, Kim shouts, "Michael, stop! Turn around, and look at me." When I don't respond, she loudly repeats, "Michael, stop!"

I obey and turn my chair in her direction. She is sitting on the table with her legs together and only the tips of her sneakers are touching the floor. As I wheel myself closer, she leans forward with her hands clutching the edge of the table. "I know you don't want to hear this, but it's time for you to go," she says. "You have made an outstanding recovery, Michael."

"Kim, you don't understand! In here, I feel normal. I'm accepted for who I am. But beyond these walls, I don't know how others will treat me. Speaking from experience, I know how cruel and judgmental people can be." I pause momentarily then continue. "Before I got injured, I knew who I was and what I wanted to do with my life: I was an athlete, and I wanted a career teaching tennis. But now, I can barely put one foot in front of the other, so it's scary to even contemplate what my future holds."

"You're going home to family and friends, and you'll continue to improve. So just put your fears aside and embrace your future!" Kim's reply unintentionally defuses the tension in the conversation.

"How did you know I'm going to stay with my parents? I just found out last night!"

"Your dad saw me in the hallway last week as I was leaving to go home. He told me then," she admits.

"Why does that not surprise me?" I retort.

Looking me square in the eyes, Kim says, "Listen to me. You are one of the few quads who will walk out of this place. Never forget that. You have bigger and better things to do than hang around here for the rest of your life!" Then she adds with a smile, "Besides, all of us around here are tired of seeing you in those tights and pedaling that damn stationary bike all morning long." With that comment, we both chuckle.

The next day, my parents and I meet with Dr. Alsentzer, and he confirms that I'll be discharged on Friday, February 21.

CHAPTER 14

The rest of the week, I stay true to my motto by working hard and playing hard from sunup to sundown. I've gained enough strength in my legs that I no longer need the handrails in the hallway to make my way around the rehab center. Each day, I make a concerted effort to find my favorite staffers and engage them in friendly games of tennis. I spend quality time with Mike, Marty, and Lenny, who have become true friends.

During physical therapy, Kim challenges me one more time to take as many steps as possible. I can tell my legs are getting stronger every day, but my ability to balance is still a problem.

I also relish my time in recreational therapy. Spending time with Jim Barrett is a blessing. His selfless acts of kindness have benefited all of us. In occupational therapy, now that I know my departure date, I put the finishing touches on my mug, which reads 11-19-1985 to 2-21-1986. I decide the dates on my gold bracelet will match the dates on my mug.

On Thursday, February 20, I wake up to my last full day in the rehab center, and I'm determined to finish strong. For the last time, my feet are strapped to the pedals of the dilapidated stationary bike. After I make my last rotation of the pedals, I say a prayer of thanksgiving to God for this bike. Like me, it's a flawed piece of equipment, and I pray God uses me—a guy who's imperfect in every way—to perfectly execute his plan for my life when I leave this place.

On Friday, February 21, Father Time catches up to me. His hourglass is empty, and it's time for me to go. The get-well balloons have long since deflated, and the cards have been packed away for weeks. As I leave my room, I take one last shot at my basketball hoop. When Mama asks if I want to take it with me, I tell her I'm going to leave it here so that hopefully someone else can get as much enjoyment from it as I did. With a final glance back, I leave my room dressed in street clothes with two items in my lap: my ceramic mug, which is fresh out of the kiln, and Arnold the lion.

Then my parents and I make our way around the rehab center to say both thank you and goodbye to all the people who have touched my life here. We track down Mike, Marty, and Lenny, and I make my farewells with promises to keep in touch. Next, we stop by Dr. Duncan's office so I can thank him for lending a caring ear and providing sound advice. We briefly talk with Dr. Alsentzer and Mike Bousman and thank them for keeping me healthy. I specifically thank Dr. A for allowing me to stay in my wheelchair in the evenings so I could continue to exercise.

We leave the administration office and travel the short distance to Jim Barrett's office. He rarely spends time there, but as we get closer, I see that his door is open. As I roll into his office, I say, "Knock. . . . I just wanted to stop by and say goodbye."

He turns around, smiles, and looks at us with those sparkling brown eyes. "We are really going to miss you around here," he says fondly.

I wheel my chair closer to him and extend both hands. "Will you help me up?" I ask. He grabs my hands and pulls me to a standing position. Then I wrap my arms around his torso and give him my best hug. "Thank you for everything," I whisper as my halo rests on his shoulder.

CHAPTER 14

"My pleasure," he replies, smiling. "We've had some good times, haven't we?"

"Yes, we have," I say. "I'll stop by when I come to outpatient therapy."

"You better!" he says.

From his office, we make our way down to physical therapy so I can say goodbye to Kim. As we enter through the doors, Kim is working with a patient who's lying on a padded table near the front entrance. I make my way over to the table, while my parents wait by the door.

"Hey, I just wanted to stop in and say goodbye," I say.

She steps away from her patient and walks over to me. "I was hoping to get to your room early this morning and say goodbye, but things got hectic around here," she says apologetically.

"No worries. Can you help me up one last time?" I ask with my arms extended.

"Sure," she says with a smile. "But this isn't the last time I'll help you up. I'll see you next week for outpatient therapy."

"I know, but it won't be the same," I reply.

Kim helps me to my feet, and we embrace. I don't want to let her go, but I do. "The words *thank you* feel so inadequate, but those are the only words I can find."

"You're welcome," she says. "You made my job easy."

Kim helps me sit back down in my wheelchair, and we make our way over to the entrance. I fight off tears as Kim greets my parents and hugs them goodbye. As my parents and I head out the door, Kim reminds me that she'll see me next week.

Our last stop is to say goodbye to my archnemesis, Althea. I'm not surprised to find her going door-to-door distributing medications to patients. I greet her in the hallway by saying, "Althea, this is your lucky day! You're finally getting rid of me!"

She scoffs and shakes her head. "Not as lucky as the custodial staff. They'll be thrilled to know the hallway baseboards won't need cleanin' tonight!" she cackles.

Her sassy comeback makes me laugh. As Daddy helps me to my feet, my legs are already shaking from fatigue, but they hold me steady while I give Althea a big hug. With my arms wrapped around her, I whisper, "Thank you for allowing this southern boy to fulfill a dream." Then I squeeze her a little tighter to let her know just how much she means to me and to make sure she knows that *I* know she went far above and beyond the call of duty for me. Nursing can be a thankless job, but I hope that's not the case for Althea today.

As we pull away from each other, Althea breaks the sappy moment as only she can. "Now that you're leavin' maybe I can drop the five pounds I've gained from all the M&M's you've been forcin' me to eat!" Despite her grin, I can hear the emotion in her voice.

My parents let Althea know how much they appreciate all she has done for me, and she hugs them both. She lives on the outskirts of Washington, so we make a promise to stop by and take her out to lunch one day.

Having completed my farewells, Daddy pushes me toward the main lobby as Mama follows behind carrying a duffel bag of my belongings. Rolling down the hall, I take one last look at the large wooden handrails that have my fingerprints all over them.

CHAPTER 14

Eventually, we reach the lobby, and through the large glass windows, I see a couple of nurses eating a late breakfast or perhaps an early lunch in the common area. It doesn't seem very long ago that I arrived paralyzed on a stretcher and looked out these same windows wondering what rehab would be like.

Daddy parks my chair near the front entrance and goes to get the car. As I sit with my stuffed lion and mug in my lap, I gaze down at the dates on the cup. The turbulent journey I've traveled between those two dates has left an indelible mark on my memory.

During that time, my viewfinder has served many purposes: It's been my protector when reality was too scary. It's both convicted and enlightened me and taught me powerful lessons about empathy. The viewfinder rekindled a deep love for my family and strengthened my faith in God by allowing the Holy Spirit to transform my heart.

Shifting my eyes from the mug to my lion, I can truthfully say that I have taken Arnold Schwarzenegger's advice: I have taken each day one day at a time, and I have fought hard to rebuild my body. Have I been as brave as a lion? No, I have not. Thankfully I—and all those who believe in Christ—know that "For when I am weak, then I am strong." (2 Cor. 12:10). The more important question that faces me now is: will I bravely move forward and find my purpose in life?

Suddenly, the double doors to the rehab center open, and Daddy walks in. Behind him, I see the family car waiting to take me home but also to take me away from a place that has become like a home. As Mama starts to push me toward the exit, I grab the wheels to my chair and tell her to stop. She quickly removes her hands from the back of the wheelchair as if she's touched a hot stove.

"What's going on?" Daddy asks as he sees Mama step back from the wheelchair.

"There's something I need to do," I say as I lock the wheels to my chair.

"What do you need to do?" he responds, his eyebrows raised with curiosity.

"Walk out of here," I reply with a mix of caution and confidence.

My father looks at me with surprise and advises, "Son, that's not a good idea."

Looking back at him, I say, "Maybe not, but it's a *brave* idea, and right now, I need to be brave."

I lean down, tighten my AFO braces, and swivel the footrests of my chair out of the way. I hand Arnold and the mug to Mama, and Daddy helps me stand. Then Mama unlocks my wheelchair and brings it around in front of me. With only mild trepidation, I grab the handles to my wheelchair, and on February 21, 1986, ninety-four days after the accident that left me paralyzed from the neck down, I walk out of Pitt County Regional Rehabilitation Center.

CHAPTER 14

THE VIEWFINDER

Dressed for my acting debut in the movie, *Raw Deal*

My beloved Baja Bug

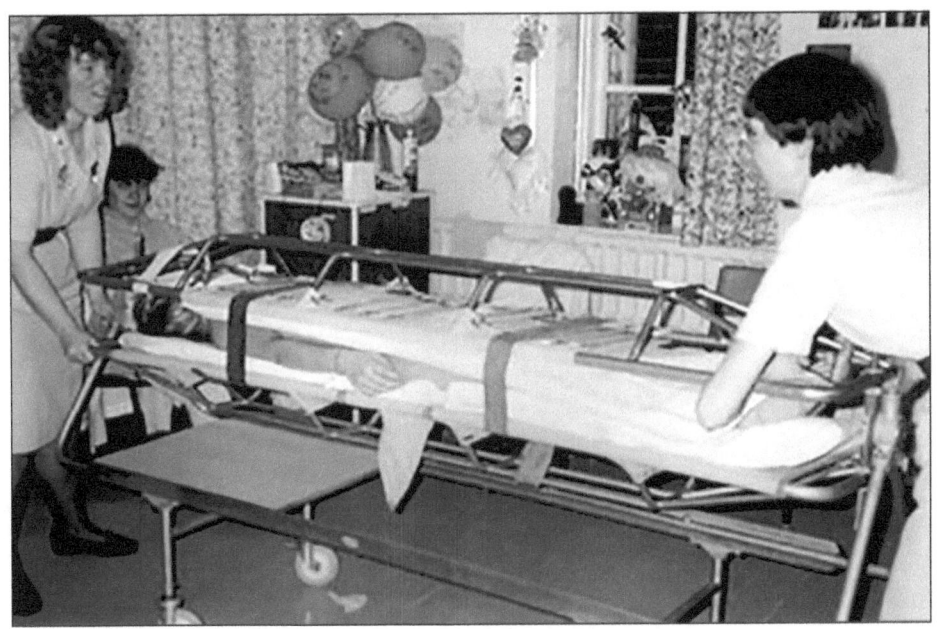

Stryker frame traction bed—no, that's not me

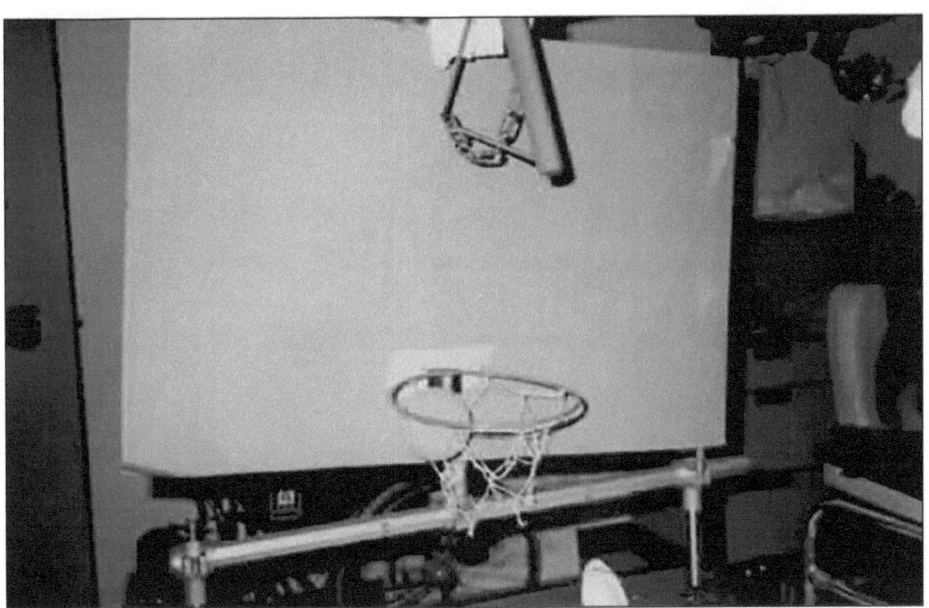

My worn-out basketball goal

THE VIEWFINDER

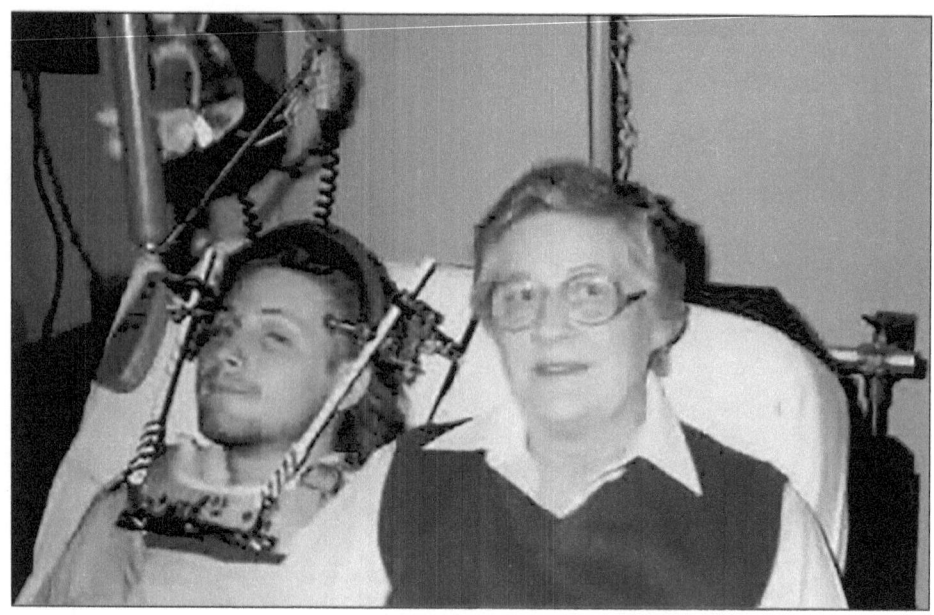

Mama and me

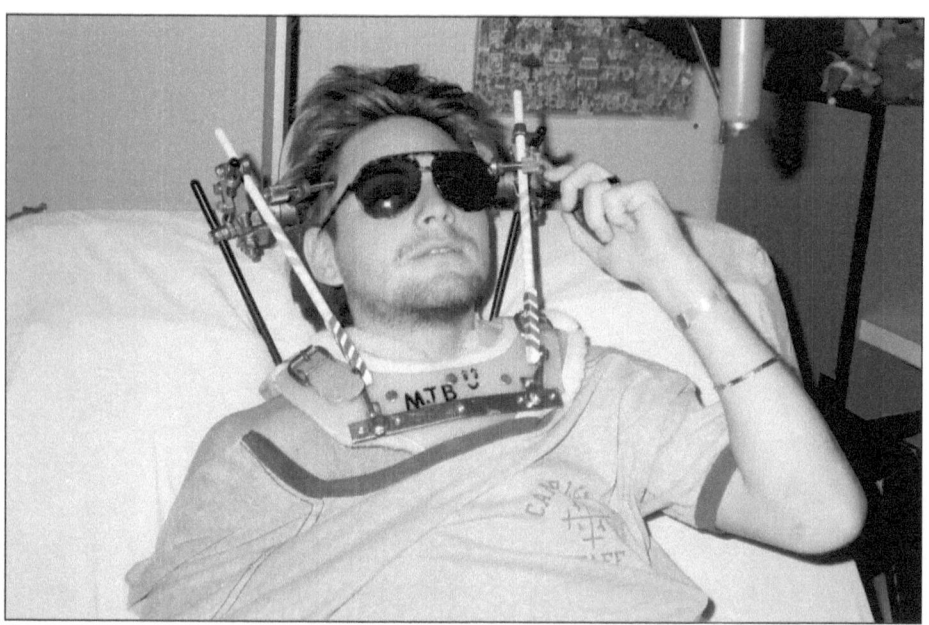

Pixie Stix colored halo rods

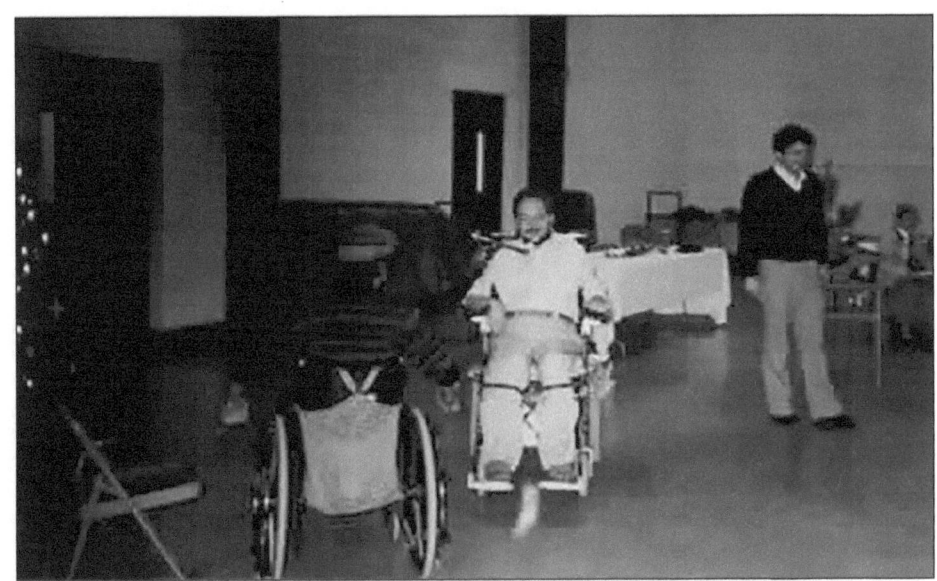

Marty Silverstone (C), Jim Barrett (R), and Mike Hamer with his back to the camera

Mike Hamer and his hammered dulcimer and harmonica

THE VIEWFINDER

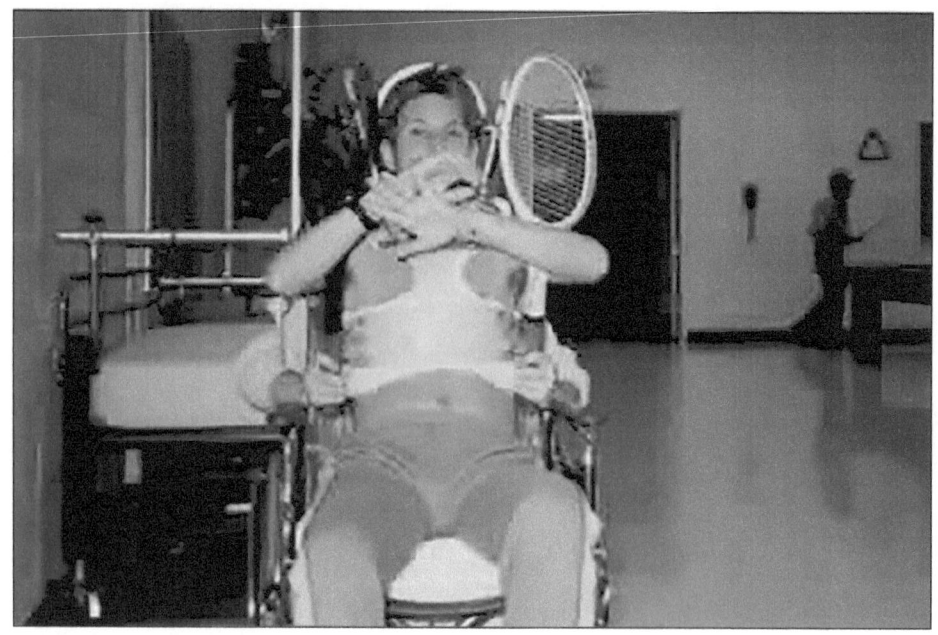

Goofing around with Sharon after a competitive game of "volley" tennis

Arnold the Lion and the cup I painted in occupational therapy

Taking a stroll around Washington Park

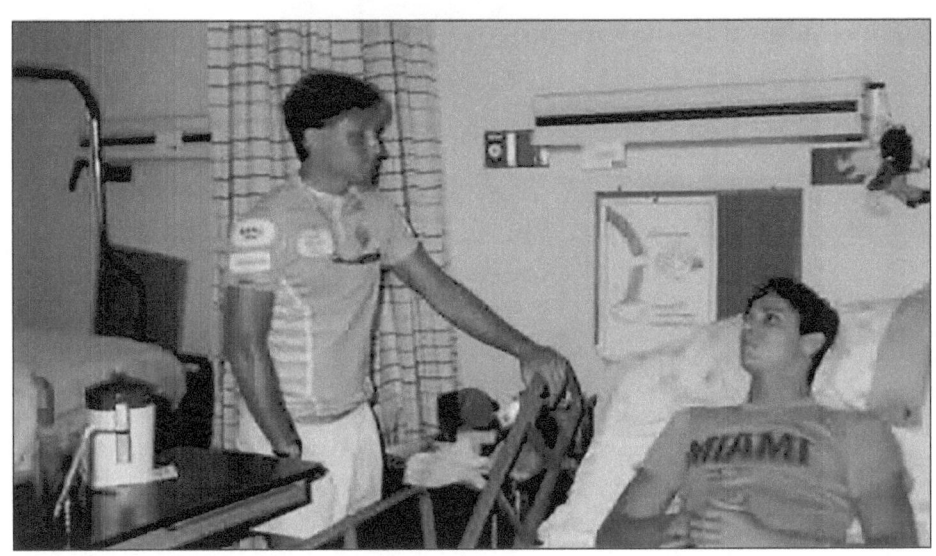

Visiting a patient at Memorial Hospital and Rehab Center, Jacksonville, FL, on Ride to Recovery I (1986)

THE VIEWFINDER

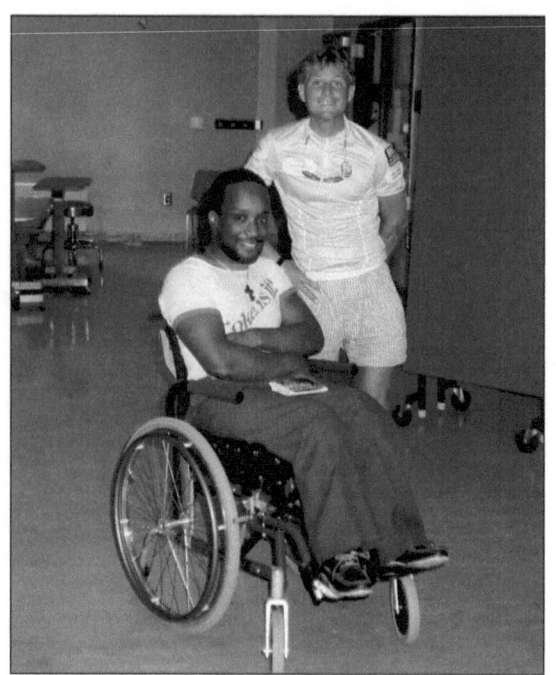

Surprise meeting with my friend, Lenny, while visiting Shepard's Spinal Center in Atlanta, GA, on Ride to Recovery I (1986)

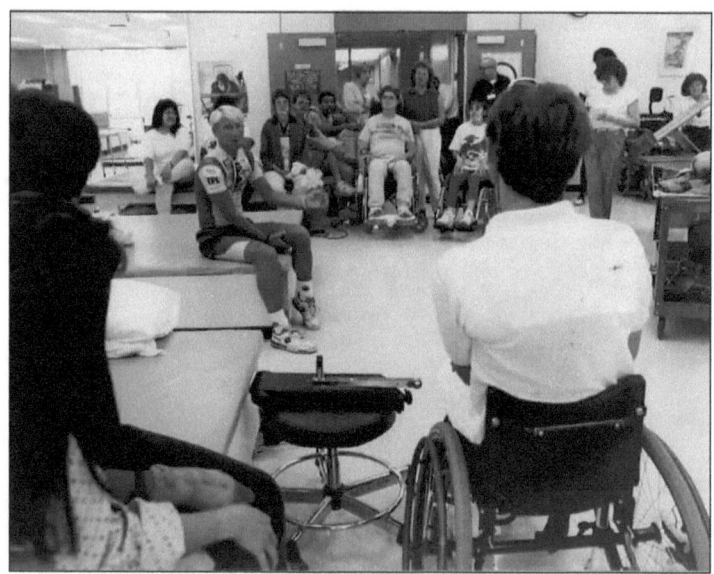

Sharing my story with patients at Cosa Colina Rehab Center, Pomona, CA, on Ride to Recovery II (1989)

Arriving at our final destination—Daniel Freeman Hospital two months and two weeks after leaving Wilmington, NC, on Ride to Recovery II (1989)

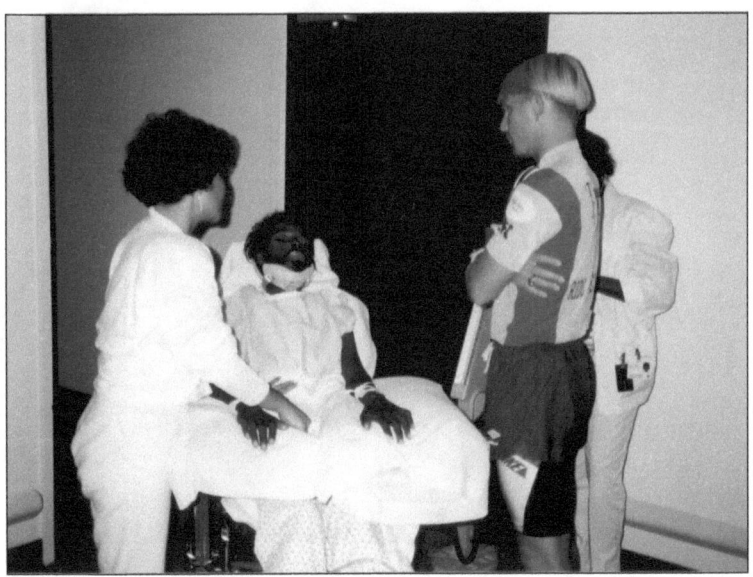

Visiting a newly injured patient at Daniel Freeman Hospital, Inglewood, CA (1989)

THE VIEWFINDER

Pedaling uphill to Woodrow Wilson Hospital and Rehab Center, Fisherville, VA, on Ride to Recovery III (1991)

Visiting the National Spinal Cord Injury Headquarters, Woburn, MA, on Ride to Recovery III (1991). (L-R) Paul Pagano, Dolores McLean, me, and Rebecca Robinson

Mount Olive Junior College Tennis Team (1982) (Top L-R) Kermit Nixon, Paul Pagano, David McGee (Bottom L-R) Me, Danny Phillips, Jean Scaturo, and Tom Cogins

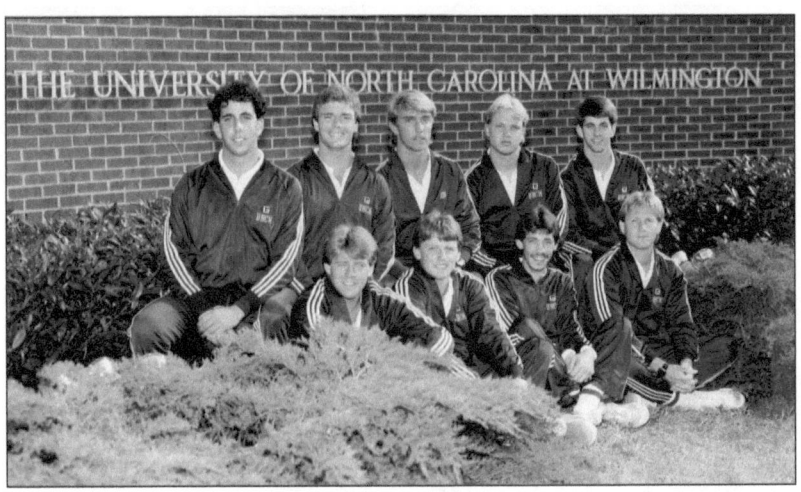

UNC-Wilmington Tennis Team (1984) (Top L-R) Steve Marer, David McGee, Brad Cheers, Slate Thompson, and Tommy Allen (Bottom L-R) Terry Gratz, Jeff Rock, Kermit Nixon, and me

THE VIEWFINDER

Hoggard Tennis Team (2014)

My "archnemesis" and dear friend, Althea Carboni (2021)

Kim Hall and her son, Josh (1995)

Recreational therapist, Jim Barrett (2021)

The Bowen Family, Christmas (1974)

THE VIEWFINDER

Betty and Bo Bowen at our wedding rehearsal (1996)

My brother Lee and me (2009)

Laura Lee and me (2020)

Painted by: Betty P. Bowen—Her Favorite!

Painted by: Christopher M. Bowen

EPILOGUE

In mid-March 1986, Dr. Hardy and Dr. Anthony quarreled over who was responsible for removing my halo. After wearing the contraption for four months, my parents and I made the trip to New Hanover Regional Medical Center, where Dr. Anthony removed my halo. It was such a relief not having that weighty gizmo screwed to my head anymore. When the halo was removed, I was shocked that I didn't have the muscle strength to hold up my head. Thank God for the neck brace.

In April, even though I was going to outpatient therapy three times a week and taking daily strolls around the block in Washington Park, I struggled with learning how to walk in braces while using a walker. However, my walking woes would improve after an accidental encounter with a relic in my parents' garage.

On that particular day, I was heading out for my morning walk and needed a clean sweatshirt. Mama told me to grab one out of the dryer in the garage. Our garage was basically just layers upon layers of clutter, and while squatting down to reach into the dryer, I saw a bicycle tire peeking out from underneath a tarp. I

EPILOGUE

recognized the fat front tire: it was from Daddy's German-made World War II–era bicycle. My brother used this bike in 1970 when he attempted to get his name in the *Guinness Book of World Records* for jumping over eleven aluminum trash cans. He made it across eight cans before landing on trash can number nine and flattening it into a pancake.

I cleaned up the bike, and suppressing my rational thoughts that told me this was a bad idea, I took off my braces, put down my cane, and mounted the bicycle seat. After a shaky start, I gained my balance and was off to the races pedaling down Fairview Avenue. It was a liberating experience as the bicycle freed me from my disability.

After a week of riding my dad's bike, I purchased a twelve-speed road bike and realized the therapeutic benefits. The toe clips on the pedals of my bike allowed me to strap my feet in and subdue my spastic ankles. My right hand was still nonfunctional at this point, but when I pedaled, it closed and gripped the handlebar. In a sense, it contributed to my success controlling the bike rather than hindering me. Soon, the highlight of my daily therapy routine became cycling around Washington Park. Surprisingly, the more I biked, the less spastic my muscles were, which, in turn, allowed me to be more fluid when I walked. In the span of a month, I went from biking a mile a day to ten miles a day.

That same spring of 1986, Sharon and I attended a meeting at Pitt County Regional Rehabilitation Center. Several former patients and current staff members were interested in creating a local chapter of the National Spinal Cord Injury

Association (NSCIA). During the meeting, we were all tossing around proposals of how to raise money for the chapter. Without discussing it with my parents or Sharon, I blurted out, "I'm planning a bicycle trip to visit rehabilitation centers along the East Coast. I can turn the trip into a fundraiser for the chapter."

Out of the corner of my eye, I noticed Sharon looking at me in disbelief. When the meeting concluded, she took me aside. Bemused, she asked, "When did you plan this bicycle trip? And when were you going to tell me about it?"

"I haven't. There is no plan," I told her. "It's just an idea that came to me during the meeting."

Eventually, my parents and Sharon got on board with the idea. Sharon and I sent out hundreds of letters asking for donations from businesses and prominent people in eastern North Carolina to fund our trip and support the newly established NSCIA chapter. I trained for two and a half months, and on August 1, Sharon and I departed from Pitt County Regional Rehabilitation Center on a quest to visit six rehab facilities. Sharon dubbed the trip "Ride to Recovery." Accompanying me in Daddy's pickup truck, she navigated via bike maps while I cycled from Greenville to Jacksonville, Florida, covering more than five hundred miles in the process.

Our mission was twofold. First, we wanted to raise awareness of and money for the newly founded Eastern Chapter of the National Spinal Cord Injury Association. Second, we wanted to deliver a simple message of encouragement to patients through my motto: "Take one day at a time. All day long, do your very best, and let God worry about the rest." My goal was to motivate patients to develop a work ethic

EPILOGUE

that would produce the best possible outcome. If they did this, at the end of their time in rehab, they could leave with no regrets.

About midway through the trip, severe saddle sores started bothering me. The sores brought on painful muscle spasms that hampered my ability to bike the daily distances needed to stay on schedule. But I had to practice the very message I was delivering to patients, so I gave it my best effort on the bike every day and didn't worry about my inability to meet my daily mileage goals. Despite my lackluster performance on the bike, my message and story radiated with both patients and staff at each of the facilities we visited.

After returning from our trip in September 1986, I moved back to Wilmington and reenrolled at UNCW to finish my degree in phys ed and complete my student teaching. I do not believe it was a coincidence that out of all the student interns in my class, I was the student assigned to a supervising teacher who taught adaptive phys ed. So my student teaching involved working with kids of all ages with a wide range of disabilities. I'll be forever grateful that my professors, supervising teacher, and students were sympathetic to the change in my abilities. The following May, I graduated with a degree in physical education.

In September 1987, Dr. Simmons, the principal at Lake Forest Junior High School in Wilmington, took a chance and hired me as a phys ed teacher even though my residual paralysis was on full display. The following year, Lake Forest Junior High closed, and I transferred to the newly built Myrtle Grove Middle School.

THE VIEWFINDER

In December 1987, Sharon and I attended the Urbana World Missionary Conference at the University of Illinois–Urbana-Champaign. She needed to know if God was calling her to do missionary work overseas, and I was there to support her. In one of the breakout sessions at the conference, I talked to a missionary group from Hong Kong that was recruiting college tennis players to share the gospel of Jesus Christ through teaching tennis. Although this mission sparked my interest, I didn't feel that God was calling me to travel halfway around the world to share the gospel. Just as important, I was a "walking quadriplegic" who had no ability to teach tennis.

The highlight of the conference for me was meeting Joni Eareckson Tada, whose life story I so admired. A brief conversation with her literally changed the direction of my life. During the conference, she gave an inspirational talk about her missionary work with Joni and Friends, an organization that advocates for those with disabilities. Afterward, I told her about my accident and my recent bicycle trip visiting rehab centers. When she asked if I was interested in missionary work overseas, I told her no, that I didn't feel a calling to do missionary work abroad. But her response stuck with me. "It's just as important to do missionary work here at home as it is abroad," she said.

On the bus ride back to North Carolina, I thought about Joni's statement. Just like the words, "take it one day at a time" radiated from Arnold Schwarzenegger's mouth, Joni's recommendation to do missionary work here at home planted a seed inside me. *Maybe God's purpose in me attending this missionary conference was not to*

EPILOGUE

serve him abroad, I thought to myself, *but to realize I need to serve him closer to home.*

That January, I returned to Wilmington and Sharon resumed classes at ECU. But soon, she stopped writing affectionate letters and our lengthy phone calls grew few and far between. Unbeknownst to me, Sharon's faith was taking her in a direction that didn't include me. Finally, late on a Sunday afternoon in the spring of 1988, Sharon called to tell me goodbye. Heartbroken, I channeled all my physical and emotional energy into training.

Breaking up with Sharon motivated me to do my missionary work here at home. My plan was to bicycle across America to inspire those with spinal cord injuries to never give up and give all the glory to God. From the spring of 1988 to the summer of 1989, I took my work ethic to another level. When I wasn't teaching phys ed, I could be found at the health club lifting weights or logging miles on my new custom-made road bike.

In 1988, while teaching at Myrtle Grove Middle School, I befriended two God-fearing teachers: Rebecca Robinson Clark and Dolores McLean. I let them in on my goal of bicycling across America and asked them to help me fulfill this dream. Deep down, I knew that recruiting these two selfless women to travel across the country and help individuals who have suffered spinal cord injuries would be a blessing to so many others.

Like me, Rebecca was a phys ed teacher. I noticed right away that her height and physical strength equaled her spiritual strength in Christ. Her personality was (and is) a blend of optimism, humor, and compassion for others. Drafting behind Rebecca produced a slipstream that any race car driver would appreciate. In a letter she sent me in the summer of 2018, she used the following quote (author unknown) to describe our forever friendship:

> In life, you realize there is a role for everyone you meet. Some will test you, some will use you, some will love you, and some will teach you. But the ones who are truly important are the ones who bring out the best in you. They are the rare and amazing people who remind you why it's worth it.

Dolores had (and still has) a spiritual light to her personality that's contagious. On our rehab visits, I often saw her off to the side listening to a patient or a parent talking about how their son or daughter was injured. While interacting with families, her demureness was always on full display, and when it came to getting us from one rehab center to the next, she was masterful. Dolores's ability to decipher thousands of miles of bicycling maps took patience and talent. She understood that making mistakes costs Rebecca and me valuable energy. Needless to say, she rarely made a mistake.

On June 10, 1989, Ride to Recovery II began. Rebecca and I mounted our bikes and set out on a journey to bicycle from Wilmington to Los Angeles, California. Under Dolores's watchful eyes and direction, we crisscrossed the United States visiting nineteen rehabilitation facilities where I shared my success story. It was an inspirational message of encouragement without providing false hope, and I delivered it to hundreds of patients and staff members. Along the

EPILOGUE

way, we experienced America like few people do, cycling across the scenic Blue Ridge Mountains, through the Great Plains of Kansas, and over the breathtaking Rockies in Colorado. We trekked across the rugged terrains of Utah and through the oppressive Mojave Desert in Nevada and California. Every day, we set out to do our very best. Some days we reached our target distance; other days we didn't. But Rebecca and I pushed each other to our physical limits. And with every patient we met, the three of us offered love, compassion, and empathy: virtues the viewfinder revealed to me during my rehabilitation.

On August 2, 1989, Rebecca and I pedaled into Inglewood, California, with Dolores right on our tail. A police escort guided us to our final destination: the Daniel Freeman Rehabilitation Hospital. We received a hero's welcome with crowds of people cheering and TV cameras rolling. It was a day that I'll never forget.

After the trip, I fell back into my role as a public school phys ed teacher with no plans of ever getting back on a bicycle. However, those of you who live by faith know that God sometimes has other plans. In 1990, a recurring thought infiltrated my bedtime prayers: *There is more work to do.* I tried unsuccessfully to rationalize this thought away, telling myself that I had already talked with hundreds of patients and bicycled thousands of miles. But the thought would not go away! I'd visited rehab hospitals down the East Coast and across the country. The only other avenue was to travel north. *Is God telling me to head north?* I wondered.

I got the answer one day while straightening up my apartment. I came across a catalog that I'd used to contact rehab centers on both of my previous cycling trips. Colored tabs earmarked the pages of the rehab centers we'd visited. As I thumbed through the booklet, the name Woodrow Wilson Rehabilitation Center caught my eye. *Where have I seen that name before?* I asked myself. Then it hit me! Early in my recovery, my brother had videotaped a short motivational film he saw on TV about Morris E. Goodman. Nicknamed "The Miracle Man," Goodman sustained a horrific spinal cord injury in a plane crash. Against all odds, he overcame paralysis and walked out of the rehabilitation center. I watched that film many times for motivation and inspiration, and I suddenly remembered that Morris had been transferred to Woodrow Wilson Rehabilitation Center in Fishersville, Virginia.

I closed the catalog and noticed the logo and address for the headquarters of the National Spinal Cord Injury Association in Woburn, Massachusetts. I thought, *These are two significant places that mean a lot to me. I haven't visited either place, and both are north of here.*

A few days later, I contacted Janna Jacobs, the Executive Director of the NSCIA, and explained to her my interest in cycling north to visit rehab centers and the national headquarters. She said it would be great if the Ride to Recovery could end at the headquarters and receive recognition at the NSCIA national conference in August. At the end of the phone call, I felt my conversation with Janna was the answer to my recurring thought: *There's more work to do.*

On July 17, 1991, Ride to Recovery III departed from Wilmington. My message was the same one I'd delivered to patients many times before: "Take one day at a

EPILOGUE

time. All day long, do your very best, and let God worry about the rest." On this trip, I also raised money for the National Spinal Cord Injury Association. None of this would've been possible without Rebecca and Dolores, who, yet again, sacrificed much of their summer to accompany me. As a bonus, my loyal friend and college teammate Paul Pagano joined us along the way. He also understood the impact that paralysis has on a family. When Paul was a boy, his father suffered an accident at work that caused partial paralysis and left him unable to work. Paul's efforts on the bike and empathizing with patients and their families benefited the trip and also honored his father's memory.

On Ride to Recovery III, we visited six rehabilitation centers. Our first stop was Woodrow Wilson Rehabilitation Center. Although it had been over a decade since Morris Goodman had traveled the hallways of the facility, his legacy was very much alive.

As a seasoned cyclist, having trekked over the Rocky Mountains and through the Mojave Desert, I felt mentally and physically prepared for any challenge that would arise on this trip north. That feeling quickly subsided when we hit the streets of New York City. I'm not sure which was more frightening, the taxicabs cutting us off or the people in parked cars opening their doors in front of us. After a few close calls, we racked our bikes and headed to Mount Sinai Hospital and Rehabilitation Center where patients and the staff made us feel safe and welcomed.

On August 6, Ride to Recovery III concluded in Woburn, Massachusetts, at the NSCIA headquarters. The following day, at the opening ceremonies of the NSCIA

THE VIEWFINDER

national conference, I accepted a merit award acknowledging my efforts—as well as those of Rebecca, Dolores, and Paul—to improve the quality of life for those with spinal cord injuries. To me, the award signified an end to my work—at least while sitting on a bicycle seat.

Looking back, as weary as my body became pedaling mile after mile, I never grew tired of sharing my story with patients and staff. From 1986 to 1991, I visited thirty-three rehabilitation facilities throughout America and logged closed to ten thousand miles on the bike. And to think, this five-year journey started with pedaling a broken-down stationary bike and a vivid dream of cycling through the countryside. What a humbling experience to know that God used me—his imperfect servant—to serve others, and I was the greatest beneficiary. It blessed me to fulfill my dream with the help of so many good people—none more selfless than Rebecca and Dolores. There are not enough days in my lifetime to thank them for their sacrifices and altruistic acts of kindness.

In May 1991, not long before Ride to Recovery III hit the road, I was scouting a band to play at a promotional party to raise money for the journey when I met my future wife, Laura Lee Cole. After a lengthy courtship, we married in 1996. Early in our marriage, when we were looking for things to do together, I picked up a tennis racket and taught her how to play. This decision rekindled my love for the game. Although I could no longer play at the level I had before my accident, I enjoyed passing on what I'd learned from my years of playing competitively.

In August 2003, I fulfilled a dream that for so many years I believed was

EPILOGUE

impossible: I earned my professional tennis teaching certification and became a proud member of the United States Professional Tennis Association (USPTA).

In 2006, Sheila Boles, the athletic director at Hoggard High School in Wilmington, asked me to take over the men's tennis program. I accepted, and three years later, I took over the women's program as well. I felt blessed to coach so many talented young athletes, some who followed in my footsteps to play college tennis.

In 2017, I retired as the coach of the men's team and focused my attention on the women's team. Then, in January 2020, after thirty-three years as a public schoolteacher, I retired from Myrtle Grove Middle School, but I remain the women's tennis coach at Hoggard High School.

Late on the night of December 5, 1985, I prayed that God would take my life, but if it wasn't my time to be with him, I asked him to bless me with a purpose in life. He has kept his promise to me, and with a grateful, humble heart, I can say that I have kept my promise to him. I believe there is no greater purpose than being a public servant.

Teaching at a Title I public school, I've experienced all the blessings and heartbreak that I would have if I'd pursued missionary work. Throughout my teaching career, I've been blessed to teach and build a rapport with lots of kids like Trey and Annie. I've been humbled to my core teaching kids who were homeless, parentless, and penniless. For the dozens of children with physical disabilities who came through the gym doors at Myrtle Grove Middle School, it has been a nostalgic blessing to share my story with them and be their teacher. For twenty-five years,

THE VIEWFINDER

I worked alongside Bill Williams, a fellow PE teacher, to help lead a Fellowship of Christian Athlete's huddle, sharing the gospel of Jesus Christ with thousands of students.

As I reflect on my life, any positive impact that I've had on others since my accident—whether through visiting rehab centers, coaching, or teaching—I can attribute to one word: *empathy*. Through the vehicle of my spiritual viewfinder, God transformed my heart at the age of twenty-three. He placed in my heart a deep awareness for the feelings of others and a passion to help make a difference, especially in the lives of children and people with disabilities. I pray that my story has inspired you to live a life of empathy.

ACKNOWLEDGMENTS
(*) In Memoriam

To the love of my life, my wife Lauri, thank you for helping transform my words into a story. To our dog, Tessa, thank you for being my sidekick while I rewrote this book. To my parents, Walter "Bo" and Betty Patton Bowen, thank you for your unwavering love and support of me, my goals, and my aspirations.* To my grandmother, Heilda Alligood Bowen, thank you for being the Christian influence in my life when I was growing up. I long for the day when we can once again sit together on your beloved porch swing.* To my brother, Lee Bowen, thank you for being a loving big brother, my protector, and a role model growing up. To my sisters-in-law, niece, and nephews: Cyndi Bowen and Becky Bucci, Christopher, Beau, and Dylan Bowen, and Kaitlyn and Matthew Bucci, thank you for your love and support. To the Wall family, Aunt Joan and Uncle James,* and my cousins Pat, Tim, and Jennifer Wall, thank you for the influential childhood memories. To the Patton family, Uncle Ed and Aunt Judy, and my cousins Jonathan and Denise Patton, thank you for showing the Wall-Bowen family what it is to live by faith.

THE VIEWFINDER

A special thank you to my cousin Jonathan Patton, for being an inspiration to me.* To my father-in-law, Jerry "Captain" Cole, thank you for being the anchor of the Bowen–Bucci family.* To my mother-in-law, Elizabeth Cole, thank you for loving me as your son. To Sharon Creal Foster, thank you for loving me during my darkest days. To Rebecca Robinson Clark and Dolores McLean, how blessed I am to have lifelong friends who unselfishly traveled across America to help me live out my dream. Thank you from the bottom of my heart. To Sally Meserole, thank you for your steadfast friendship, for proofreading my manuscript, and for offering valuable insight on how to make it better. To Ed Hodges, thank you for inspiring me to become a teacher. To Bill Williams, my brother in Christ and loyal friend, thank you for the twenty-five years you allowed me to be part of the Fellowship of Christian Athletes at Myrtle Grove Middle School. To my band of tennis brothers—David McGee, Paul Pagano, and Kermit Nixon—thank you for all your support during the good times and bad. To the Washington Park Boys: Bill Batchelor, Todd and Tommy Buckman, Tommy Dunlap, Melvin Grant, Paul and Vance Moore, Reid Pinkham, John Robinson, and Charles Rhodes, thank you for creating so many hilarious childhood memories that they are worthy of me writing a second book. To Kim Hall, thank you for your unwavering positive attitude and for never allowing me to give up on recovery.* To Jim Barrett, thank you for your selfless personality and lifelong service to helping people with physical disabilities. To my "archnemesis" Althea, our friendship started off as oil and water but mellowed into a fine wine. Thank you for lifting me up on those days

ACKNOWLEDGMENTS

when I was beaten down. To Mike Hamer and Marty Silverstone, you made rehab tolerable. Rest in peace my friends.* To Dr. Ulrich Alsentzer, thank you for being kindhearted, for never mincing your words, and for always being straightforward with me. To Dr. Ira Hardy and Dr. Robert Turner, simply stated, thank you for saving my life. To Graham Hatcher, PhD, thank you for being the calm voice in my ear when I needed it the most. To Saul Bachner, PhD, thank you for your many years of friendship to Lauri and me.* To Arnold Schwarzenegger, thank you for your encouraging words that grew into a motto for me and so many others living with physical disabilities. To Joni Eareckson Tada, thank you for helping me discover my mission to serve the Lord through serving others with spinal cord injuries. To Deb Ellsworth, who created the Empathy Symbol, thank you for allowing me to use it on my book cover. To Jennifer Huston Schaeffer, thank you for the professional editing of my book and for helping guide me through the publishing process. To James Slate, thank you for taking my vision of a book cover and creating an aesthetic masterpiece.

THE VIEWFINDER

NOTE TO MAMA
May 8, 2005

Dear Mama,

As I have commented on different occasions to you and Daddy, I am amazed at the lack of parental guidance I see afforded to today's children. I remind myself that what I experience daily in education I am comparing to my own personal upbringing. It's during these moments that I realize the sacrifices you and Daddy made so Lee and I could have a better life.

It's because of these sacrifices—too many to mention—that you can be proud of raising two sons who are educated and respected in their communities and their occupations. You have been a role model teaching us the virtues of a hard day's work, the importance of honesty and humility, and the realization that although it's nice to be important, it is more important to be nice.

Me and Lee's success is a direct consequence of your and Daddy's tough love—a lost art in today's society. Growing up as a family, we all did without some of the nicer things in life. For Lee and me, it forced us to use our imaginations. Instead of buying Lee the gizmos and gadgets he wanted, it forced him to build, take apart, destroy, and reinvent the toys we played with as children. Fostering this creativity

NOTE TO MAMA

throughout his childhood and adolescence was no doubt a contributing factor to his success today. How many children's lives and homes across the country are safer now because of the products he and Cyndi have designed and manufactured?

I can attribute my success as a college tennis player and teaching pro to the countless hours I spent as a kid hitting dead tennis balls against the municipal building wall while imagining I was playing the greats of Borg and McEnroe. Although I sometimes resented the fact that you and Daddy couldn't afford for me to take tennis lessons and play in tennis tournaments, I understood the reason, and it gave me the chip on my shoulder that I needed as a player to be a winner.

On this Mother's Day, I'd like you to know that during each of the cross-country bicycle treks I embarked on, I shared with patients, parents, and rehab staff the unconditional love I received from you and Daddy. They asked me many times how my parents handled the early stages of my injury. My answer was always the same: My father stopped working to be by my bedside every night, and my mother raised me twice. At twenty-three, I became as helpless as an infant. At the time of my discharge from the rehabilitation center, when the staff gave you and Daddy the option of transferring me to a nursing home, you quickly clarified that I was going to be taken care of at home. It was you, Mama, who took care of my basic needs, so as an adult, I had the unique opportunity to experience the unconditional love a mother has for the well-being of her child. There is nothing I could ever buy you or say to you that will express my gratitude. All I can do is what I've tried to do over the past twenty years, love you—both of you! Happy Mother's Day!

THE VIEWFINDER

TRIBUTE TO DADDY FOR HIS FUNERAL
November 30, 1925–June 23, 2019

OUR DAD NEVER forgot walking hand in hand with his parents during the early years of the Great Depression through the breadline and soup kitchen at First Christian Church to get food for dinner. The economic hardships of that time had an indelible impact on him. Throughout my father's life he lived by the Great Depression–era motto: "Use it up, wear it out, make do, or do without."

Making do was easy for Daddy. As a teenage boy, he found enjoyment in the simpler things in life, like fishing. As an only son, Daddy spent his summers fishing by his house on the banks of the Pamlico River. He had a favorite cypress tree that he would climb and sit for hours watching boats make their way up and down the river. I have to believe this is when and where his love affair with the water began.

On September 17, 1943, at the age of seventeen, Daddy's love of the water was severely tested when he answered the call of his country and left his family and beloved Pamlico River for the hostile seas of the Pacific. During World War II,

TRIBUTE TO DADDY

he served as a mineman aboard the destroyer minelayer the USS *Robert H. Smith*. What most of us read in history books, my father lived through firsthand. On the twenty-fifth of January 1945, to save the crew of a downed B-29 bomber, Daddy and his shipmates sailed into waters scattered with mines off the shores of Saipan. Weeks later, he and his shipmates bombarded the shores of Iwo Jima. Then on March 25, 1945, twenty miles off the island of Okinawa, his ship took heavy fire from two kamikaze planes. On April 21 of that same year, the USS *Robert H. Smith* shot down five kamikazes off the island of Guam.

During minesweeping operations in the East China Sea, my dad's ship received word of the Japanese surrender; the war was over. However, the crew of his ship spent the next three months doing the dangerous work of clearing mines in the Yellow Sea so our US fleet and troops could return home safely. On February 7, 1946, the USS *Robert H. Smith* made its way under the Golden Gate Bridge, bringing Daddy safely home from the war.

After returning from the service, Daddy attended ECU with aspirations of being a dentist. That quickly changed when he realized he couldn't stand the sight of blood. Although medicine was not his calling, he did find success as a thief. When he met my mom at a party, she was involved with another man and they had plans to get married. She told me, "I fell for your daddy hook, line, and sinker. He hooked me with those blues eyes, he charmed me with his witty lines, and the sinker was his ability to make me laugh." He kept her laughing for fifty-nine years.

On December 5, 1985, my daddy saved my life. Many of you here know that as a young man, I sustained a broken neck in a car accident. Three weeks into my recovery, when I became deathly ill, I made the decision to give up and prayed to die. That night, Mama and Daddy got a call from the hospital telling them I had taken a turn for the worse and to come quickly. When they arrived, I was in critical condition, on a breathing tube, and waiting for surgery to drain fluid from my lungs. After the surgery, Daddy leaned over the bed and started combing my hair with his fingers, something he'd done since I was a small boy whenever I was sick or hurt. I whispered to him and Mama, "I love you guys, but I'm tired of living like this."

Daddy abruptly left the room, but I could hear him crying in the hallway. Moments later, he returned, still visibly upset. Perhaps it was father's intuition, but he told me how much he loved me—words I hadn't heard since I was a little boy. He also said, "We've come a long way, baby, and we are not giving up now."

Hearing him say "I love you" was what I needed to keep going and not give up. Since that December night so many years ago, Daddy and I have never missed the opportunity to say "I love you" to one another.

As a grown man, I've been blessed to spend time with Daddy at his beloved Beachfront RV Park in Emerald Isle. We often sat side by side at the water's edge. Many times, he reached over and put his hand on top of mine, and, together, we just stared at the ocean. As we sat, I often wondered what his eyes were seeing. Like me, was it the beauty of the Atlantic Ocean? Or was he seeing the deadly waters of the Pacific during World War II? I don't know; I never asked him. But

TRIBUTE TO DADDY

I suspect that for many of us, Father Time washes away the bad memories and allows the fond memories to remain and flourish within us.

What I do know is that Daddy loved us very much. He loved everyone in this room in his own unique way. If he were here today, he would be humbled to tears by your presence. Shortly before Daddy passed away, I shared with him a favorite verse that I will now share with you. I told him, "You've fought a good fight, you've kept the faith, you've finished your race."

Lee and I will miss you daddy all the days of our lives, but rather than say goodbye, I'll use your favorite salutation to say, see ya in the spring.

THE VIEWFINDER

www.ingramcontent.com/pod-product-compliance
Lightning Source LLC
Chambersburg PA
CBHW032005060526
44119CB00124B/461/J